PRESCRIPTION
for the
Doctor's Wife

By

Debby Read

with

Sue Addington

dawson media

PRESCRIPTION FOR THE DOCTOR'S WIFE
© 2011 by Debby Read

ISBN-13: 978-1-935651-05-5

Cover design by Liquid Lotus, LLC

LCCN: 2010938690
Printed in The United States of America
15 14 13 12 11   1 2 3 4 5 6 7 8

Endorsments

In *Prescription for the Doctor's Wife*, Debby Read dispenses wisdom laced with humor, wrapped up in poignant stories, and tied with beautiful bows of practical advice. A doctor's wife will not only learn to survive but to thrive in their challenging role. This is good medicine!

—David Stevens, MD, MA (Ethics), Chief Executive Officer, Christian Medical & Dental Associations

I wish my wife had this book available to her years ago. While I am certain she would be blessed, I am more certain I would be a better doctor—a better person—because of the impact it would have on her!

—Gene Rudd, MD, Senior VP, Christian Medical & Dental Associations

Debby Read knows firsthand what it means to be married to a hard-working doctor. In *Prescription for the Doctor's Wife,* she shares openly from her own heart and home about the real-life struggles that we all face. I know of no other book like this one. I believe it will truly bless you and help you on your journey!

—Robin Morgenthaler, Founder, Side by Side

A doctor's wife faces unique challenges; her life is a special calling no less than her husband's. Thirty-six years of marriage to Ed has provided Debby Read with understanding of situations we medical wives all recognize. With a tender, humble heart she shares poignant stories and encourages us with truth, then offers practical steps to navigate these challenges. She reminds us the Lord has much to say to us about dealing with loneliness, disappointment, change, our tongues, finances, leadership and submission, and suffering. This is God's wisdom for enjoying your husband, for building up your marriage, and for present and eternal rewards. Enjoy!

—Sally Mitchell, wife of a physician

I thought I understood my husband's life at the hospital, especially since I had been there before. But when God gave us our beautiful daughter and I began to stay at home, I realized I didn't understand anything at all. This book is a great reminder that someone else has been there, done that, and conquered—what a great encouragement!

—Andrea Colby Reed, nurse and wife of a physician

Prescription for the Doctor's Wife should be a handbook for every wife who wishes to honor her relationship with an often-absent husband. This book deals with the realities of being a medical spouse while also honoring our unique calls as daughters of God. This book is about the life journey of one woman, but it is for all women who want a strong relationship with God to be the priority in their life.

—Rev. Sarah Sealand, wife of a resident

Having been married to a physician for thirty-five years, I am delighted that Debby has drawn on her experiences and written a book that speaks so personally to the hearts of medical wives. Debby's perspective will touch not only the wives of interns, residents, and physicians, but the relationship issues addressed in this book will strike a chord in all marriages. *Prescription for the Doctor's Wife* is filled with stories, Scriptures, and suggestions that can bring a smile, hope, and healing to women everywhere.

—Dodie Anderson, wife of a physician

This book has transformed my relationship with friends, family, husband, and most importantly, Christ. It is a book like none other with great resources and incredible biblical life applications. This book is a *must-read* that will change your life. My husband and I are extremely grateful and blessed to have met Ed and Debby during my husband's first year of medical school; without them (and God) I don't know where our marriage would be today.

—Autum Edwards, wife of a nontraditional medical student and entrepreneur

When my husband first entered medical school, I remember looking for a book on how to navigate the medical world in which we were both embarking. There were very few, if any! *Prescription for the Doctor's Wife* has been an encouragement to me as it is both specific to the needs of a medical spouse and full of hope as it challenges us to keep our eyes focused on God— the ultimate Helper, Encourager, and Lover of our lives.

—Sara Smith, wife of a medical student

Prescription for the Doctor's Wife is a *must-read* for all women married to a medical professional. It was not only thought-provoking, but also life-changing for me. I have been challenged and inspired. Debby points us to Jesus who transforms us to be the medical wives we are called to be. This book is a resource for all who need practical guidance and godly wisdom for being a support to a medical spouse.

—Corrie Margaron, wife of a clinical 4th year general surgery resident

Dedication

To my dear husband and best friend, Ed. Sharing our life and love along this journey together is a blessing beyond words.

And to my beloved son, Jon. You are missed with a longing too deep to express. Your belief in this project has kept me motivated and inspired on even the darkest of days. I am sure you are smiling now that it has been completed. I look forward to the day when we can rejoice together in heaven.

Acknowledgments

Thank You, Lord, for allowing me to be Your child. I am so grateful for the privilege You have given me to write stories of Your work in my life and in the lives of my dear sisters in Christ.

Thank you, Ed, my wonderful husband and partner. I have the utmost respect and love for you. I am so grateful to have you by my side in the joys and sorrows of this life. I could not have made it through the endeavor of this book without your amazing support. How good God has been to bless me with you and our children as my dear family!

Kristi, Kim, Jon, Jacob, and David, my precious children, you have been my most fulfilling and rewarding life's work. I am immensely thankful for your extraordinary love and patience with this mom-in-training. Your adjustments to Dad's schedule, your understanding, and your positive attitudes have motivated me to be a better person. Kristi and Kim, you have grown into women I am so proud to have among my best friends and into awesome mothers to my dear grandchildren, Megan, Lauren, and Aiden. Jon, remembering your encouragement and your excitement about this project has kept me going when I could hardly bear the pain of losing you. I believe you have been cheering me on from heaven. I love you all so much.

Thank you to Kathy Tarr, my first mentor, and countless other women who have shown me in both words and actions what it means to be a godly woman. Many of the concepts in this book have been forged in the discipling relationships God has lovingly brought my way over the years. God has truly used these sweet younger women (most of them in my Side by Side group) that I have mentored, many of them married to medical students, residents, or practicing physicians, in a profound way in my life. Their hearts for God, for their husbands, and for one another have been an enormous blessing and a great inspiration to me. Thank you Andrea, Autum, Betsy, Chrissy H., Chrissy W., Corrie, Cyndi,

DeAnna, Jenny, Kathryn, Kim, Kristin, Sara, Sarah, and Taylor for deeply touching my life.

My dear friend Sue Addington, I thank you for your wisdom, insight, and enthusiasm for this book. I am so grateful for the joy of working with you in this shared labor of love.

Thank you Tom, Karen, and Christina at Dawson Media. I greatly appreciate your assistance and expertise. It has been a pleasure to work with you.

Contents

Introduction

The life of a doctor's wife is truly a special one, with many unique joys and challenges. My own journey as a medical spouse began when, more than thirty-six years ago, I married my high-school sweetheart. The induction was swift—Ed started medical school just three days after our wedding. My wonderful husband is a godly man for whom I have the utmost respect and love, and I am so grateful for the gift of sharing life with him. But as a new medical wife, I was not prepared for the challenges we would face. There was no resource available to offer support to doctors' wives when we first started out. How I would have rejoiced then to have some help and guidance!

But ultimately, in His grace and mercy, God has been my greatest teacher. Over the years I have enjoyed some successes and have also endured many difficult "learning experiences." I have been blessed to know many doctors' wives from whom I have learned a great deal. In fact, many of the concepts and principles I will share with you were forged in the discipling relationships God brought into my life.

This book has come out of my desire to encourage women who are traveling (or will travel) this difficult path as a medical spouse. Too many women I talk to are wounded and disillusioned. Too many of us are limping through life. Too many are suffering the effects of an "attack" on the heart. Sadly, too many are giving up due to a loss of hope. And many who are still "hanging in there" are secretly longing for things to be different.

Fortunately, God always has an answer for us in His Word. Psalm 19:7 tells us that His law is perfect, reviving the soul. That is good news! For we are living with dangerously low vital signs. We are gasping for breath and are in great need of resuscitation. We desperately need God to reveal Himself to us through His Word and bring about a revival of our hearts and lives.

As I sought God for direction, He inspired me to use Psalm 19 as my blueprint for this book. The beautiful, poetic imagery and profound theology spoke deeply to my heart, and I felt led to share it with you. I suggest you begin by first reading the Psalm in its entirety, using all of your God-given senses, as though tasting a favorite food. (I love chocolate—especially dark chocolate. And when I am reading God's Word, I often like to imagine that I am savoring each morsel as though it were a small bite of chocolate, melting slowly on my tongue.) Read it slowly and meditatively, asking God to allow it to nourish every cell in your body and completely satisfy your soul.

My dear friend, Sue Addington, has come alongside me in writing this book. Her daughter is married to a young physician, now in his first year of practice. Her father-in-law is a retired medical missionary, so she has heard many stories from her husband of thirty-two years, who grew up in that doctor's home. Being familiar with life in a medical family, she is well acquainted with its joys and challenges. Sue's heart for God, her encouragement, her gifts, and her insights have been invaluable to me. Our efforts have been a shared labor of love for you.

You will discover that many of the principles and lessons that follow apply to all wives—including those in a non-medical marriage or other healthcare profession marriage—and even to husbands married to a female physician. But no matter what your individual circumstances are, may the Lord, our Rock and our Redeemer, touch you deeply as you seek His wisdom in your marriage. My prayer is that this journey will be one that glorifies God and honors our husbands. And it is my hope that the following chapters will encourage you and offer support for the highs and lows ahead. Together, let us diagnose some of the causes of our maladies and seek God for the "prescription" that we need. Let's allow the Great Physician to heal us!

Psalm 19

The heavens declare the glory of God; the skies proclaim the work of his hands. Day after day they pour forth speech; night after night they display knowledge. There is no speech or language where their voice is not heard.

Their voice goes out into all the earth, their words to the ends of the world. In the heavens he has pitched a tent for the sun, which is like a bridegroom coming forth from his pavilion, like a champion rejoicing to run his course. It rises at one end of the heavens and makes its circuit to the other; nothing is hidden from its heat.

The law of the Lord *is perfect, reviving the soul. The statutes of the* Lord *are trustworthy, making wise the simple. The precepts of the* Lord *are right, giving joy to the heart. The commands of the* Lord *are radiant, giving light to the eyes. The fear of the* Lord *is pure, enduring forever.*

The ordinances of the Lord *are sure and altogether righteous. They are more precious than gold, than much pure gold; they are sweeter than honey, than honey from the comb. By them is your servant warned; in keeping them there is great reward.*

Who can discern his errors? Forgive my hidden faults. Keep your servant also from willful sins; may they not rule over me. Then will I be blameless, innocent of great transgression.

May the words of my mouth and the meditation of my heart be pleasing in your sight, O Lord, *my Rock and my Redeemer.*

℞

Chapter 1

Seek the Creator

Name :

Age :

Address :

Date :

The heavens declare the glory of God; the skies proclaim the work of his hands.

Day after day they pour forth speech; night after night they display knowledge.

There is no speech or language where their voice is not heard.

Their voice goes out into all the earth, their words to the ends of the world.

In the heavens he has pitched a tent for the sun, which is like a bridegroom coming forth from his pavilion, like a champion rejoicing to run his course.

It rises at one end of the heavens and makes its circuit to the other; nothing is hidden from its heat.

—Psalm 19:1-6

Label ☐

Refill 0 1 2 3 4 5 PRN

Refill 0 1 2 3 4 5 PRN

N ot long ago a wonderful DVD presentation of pictures taken by the Hubble space telescope caught my attention. Words cannot adequately explain what the eye could see in those photographs. As I watched the incredible display of our vast universe, I was moved to tears. The strange and wondrous cosmic images were astounding—reminding me that God is indeed an awesome Creator. My only response was to fall to my knees and praise this magnificent God.

Our amazing God reveals Himself to us in so many awesome ways. His creation speaks of Him from the highest heights to the deepest depths. Starry skies, moonlit nights, and puffy white clouds all draw our gaze upward to view God's creative glory. Majestic mountains, flower-filled meadows, and glistening new-fallen snow all beckon us to reflect on His handiwork. The myriad rainbow colors of skin, eyes, and hair of His children, not to mention their countless voices, languages, and talents, are awe-inspiring.

The wonder of God's infinite creativity is reflected in even the tiniest details around us. Consider the human body, which our husbands spend so much time studying and treating, with its microscopic cells, intricate organ systems, and incredible brain.

God's handiwork is displayed in all its glory. His creation is too marvelous to comprehend.

All parts of His creation, great and small, speak of this awesome Creator. But are we listening? Romans 1:20 tells us, "For since the creation of the world God's invisible qualities—his eternal power and divine nature—have been clearly seen, being understood from what has been made, so that men are without excuse." Psalm 19:4 of *The Message* puts it this way, "Their silence fills the earth; unspoken truth is spoken everywhere."

Do we believe that this same God who has created the universe also has a plan for each one of us and can be trusted with every detail of our life today and tomorrow . . . forever? Can He really show us how to live in such a way as to *thrive* and not just *survive?* Do we believe that God invites us, His carefully created children, to be a part of His personal family?

I grew up in a dysfunctional home with an alcoholic mother and a father who did not know how to deal with the issues this brought to our family. My parents coped by denying the problems, thereby enabling the pain to continue. But God, in His love and mercy, reached down and began to draw me to Him. He gave me a strong sense that He would help me through and that one day, some good would come of my pain. My heart of compassion for helping hurting children began then and grew in God's crucible.

The thought of being a mom has enthralled me since my very youngest days. It began when I helped care for my siblings, grew when I babysat children in our neighborhood, became cemented in my mind when I worked in a childcare facility during college, and ultimately led to my choice of profession as a pediatric nurse. Without question I loved children. But God showed me what it really meant to be part of His *family* as He assembled our own.

God brought three children into our family in the "usual" way—by birth. Kristi, Kim, and Jon have given us great joy and have taught my husband and me a great deal more than we ever taught them. My more intense education, however, came from the two children God gave us through adoption. Jacob and David have helped me to learn immensely more about God—and myself—than I ever imagined was possible.

Choose Him

My husband was still in his residency when God really showed me my deep need for Him. I was invited to participate in a Bible study by Kathy, a resident's wife a few years older than me, and it was there that I first began to read the Bible and understand this love letter from God to me. His purposes and instructions for my life were like priceless gifts, and my heart was overflowing with gratitude. My life changed when I was adopted by the Creator of the universe—as was my husband a year later. Only God can do something that big during residency when there is little time for anything besides eating, a little sleeping, and a lot of doctoring!

I often felt God speaking to me as I studied the book of James, one of my favorite books of the Bible. James 1:27 says, "Religion that God our Father accepts as pure and faultless is this: to look after orphans and widows in their distress and to keep oneself from being polluted by the world." As I read, the phrase "look after orphans" seemed to be highlighted and in bold print. I spent time praying, and then spoke with Ed about what God was showing me. We spent several years praying and seeking God's will for our lives concerning adoption.

After a long process and many prayers, God brought two "hand-picked" children into our home to join the three "homegrown" children already there. Jacob was six at the time and David was four. These precious, emotionally scarred half-brothers taught me many things. But most important among the lessons were those I learned about becoming a child of God.

On adoption day, which occurred six months after they came to live with us, Jacob and David became our sons. They had new birth certificates, new last names, and a new "forever" family to belong to. According to both the law and the commitment of our hearts, they had all the same rights and privileges of our birth children. The problem was that they had already experienced so much trauma in their lives that they were quite reluctant to accept the joys and benefits of being part of our family. They worked very hard to be "unlovable" so that we would just "reject them and get it over with," as so many others had done in their lives.

God's unconditional love for us was the example that enabled us to try our best, in His strength and power, to unconditionally love these hurting boys. As we loved Jacob and David, He loved them through us. We offered them everything we had to offer and yet they rejected our love and refused to attach to the family. It was acceptable to eat our food and sleep in our shelter, but it was not okay to do anything that would require their hearts to be involved. It was their choice, and no one else could force them to choose otherwise. Our hearts were broken as we experienced their rejection of our love and of our home. Their rebellion was discouraging. Their refusal to trust was devastating—for them and for us.

From the earliest challenges we faced in reaching out to Jacob and David, God gently reminded me of *my* rebellion to His ways, *my* refusal of His provision, *my* rejection of His love, and *my* unwillingness to act like His daughter. His gentle prodding beckoned me to deal with the times when I personally strayed from His ways. He tenderly invited me to become more like my Savior.

Lovingly, God has offered us the gift of being a part of His family. He sent His Son as a sacrifice for our sins so that we could rightly be related to Him. He desires to love us and lavish on us all the privileges of being part of His family. Why is it so hard to accept this gift? Why would anyone choose to refuse the greatest gift ever given?

Why would we become a child of the King, and then choose to live like a pauper? Jacob and David helped me to see so many times when I did not live like a child of God and did not embrace the joy, the power, the peace, the hope, and the blessings of being a daughter of the King. It was their choice to reject being part of the family. It was also their loss. Jacob has yet to accept us after eighteen years. We have an ongoing relationship with him, but it is not close. David made the life-changing decision to accept God and us, as his family, twelve long years after coming to live with us. We praise God for His faithfulness in David's life. It made all the difference as he trusted Jesus and then us. He is currently serving God and country in Iraq.

How about you? Have you chosen to be a child of God? To trust Him, who created you, with every part of your life? To have faith that He has redeemed you? To have the hope that He will bring "beauty from the ashes" of your life (Isaiah 61:3)? To rest in His power and His promises for your life?

My adopted sons showed me the difference between giving my whole heart to my Father and living for myself—independent, trusting no one, totally lost, hopeless, and all alone. We have that choice to make every day . . . to live as His child . . . or not. It may often seem like the harder path to do things His way, but it truly is the easier and better way. Let's encourage each other on this journey to remember who our Father is and why that makes all the difference in this world and the next. Let's trust Him and do life His way.

Trust in Him

As women who have the high calling of being a medical spouse, it is crucial that we understand how to become a child of God and then how to live like one. We simply cannot do this on our own. Trust me, I have tried at times and it is a disaster.

God has placed many godly women along my path that I am so grateful for. I have learned so much from them. What a great blessing and privilege it is to pass on to other women what I have learned from God and from the faithful women walking the road of life before me. Not long ago, I received a call from one of the dear women I have the privilege of mentoring. She attends the Side by Side Bible study group that I lead, which is specifically designed for women whose spouses are either studying for or practicing in the medical field.

Melissa was in tears as she shared that she needed to talk, to ask for advice, and to have me pray for her. She then told me how the strain of residency seemed to be causing so much tension in her marriage.

An important agreement I have made with the other women in our group is that there is to be no "husband bashing." Melissa knew, however, that it was certainly appropriate to discuss circumstances that are difficult for us as long as we look for our part in causing the problem and for what we can do to change ourselves to improve the situation. This dear woman had the right heart, wanting to do things God's way.

Melissa told me, "The argument and tension is my fault . . . mostly. I have let resentment of my husband's time away build up."

She felt like she needed to apologize to her husband for things she had said in anger, but was uncertain he would even call her back from the hospital. She recognized that she was being self-centered in the relationship and not pleasing God with her responses. Her description of "feeling no peace and joy" sounded quite familiar. I was impressed and touched by her desire to honor God and her husband. It is not easy when we feel overwhelmed by all of the stress, especially when it seems that there is no end in sight. You know the scenario well. A molehill, bit by bit, turns into a mighty mountain. How? Easy! Let me paint the well-known picture for you.

You may be trying to meet the needs of young children as a single parent most of the time. Then one of life's little surprises come, like seeing the beautiful snow falling outside your window—when the realization sinks in that you will have to be the one to shovel the driveway. This is followed by becoming ill with a cold after getting run down—all the while knowing your husband is busy caring for sick people but can't care for you. In addition, there is the burden of knowing that all of the shopping and gift-wrapping for the holidays is just one more thing on your plate—with no one to help. Then, your expectations for the perfect family Christmas crumble to pieces as you digest the news that your husband will not be home until late on Christmas day—if he gets home at all.

Yes, Melissa had much heartache to cry about. I had been there and understood. Sometimes that is just what we need most, someone to listen who understands and cares. We need someone who will really hear our struggles and pray for us. Then that person can point us to the One who gives us hope and reminds us that we will make it through these trials.

When our husbands do have some time for us, we hate to spend those precious moments discussing conflicts. Yet we need to talk to him at some point. It surely is difficult to know how or when to discuss these issues when our time together is so limited. We must discern what issues we need to talk God about and leave with Him and which ones we should take to our spouse. We need a right attitude and honest confession about "our part" in the conflict.

Melissa was correct when she stated that the issue was really between her and God. She was not allowing the Holy Spirit to be in control of her life. She was able to articulate the anguish of living her way and the problems that her self-focus was causing in her life and her marriage.

She realized that she needed to spend time getting things right with God, and then with her husband. She reminded herself of the need to trust her loving Creator, remembering that His heart's desire was for her greatest good. He dearly loved her, was in absolute control, and would help her through this difficult time and those to come. She was reminded of her calling as a medical wife, as a helpmate, and as a partner with her husband in his calling as a doctor.

Melissa and I had talked often about Satan's desire to destroy our marriages. How crucial it is to be aware of the threat from the Enemy of our souls. Your enemy is not your husband. It bears repeating: "The Enemy is the enemy, not my husband!" This statement had really helped her to regain perspective. We also discussed practical ways to minimize stress in our lives. Now Melissa had a plan that gave her hope and renewed commitment to God and to her husband.

It wasn't long before things began to change in Melissa's life. Though it had been hard to humble herself (as it is for all of us) and ask forgiveness, she was already seeing the many ways God was blessing this choice to trust and obey Him. One big change—praying together with her husband—had been hard to initiate, but wonderfully healing.

The insight she gained as she listened to her husband was awesome! He shared with her how he did not have time to build relationships and that often she was the only one in his life that he could talk to. "I need you," he said. "I need you to be with me and not against me." Such a powerful reminder to us as medical spouses!

Melissa was putting Ephesians 4:22-24 into action: "You were taught, with regard to your former way of life, to put off your old self, which is being corrupted by its deceitful desires, to be made new in the attitude of your minds; and to put on the new self, created to be like God in true righteousness and holiness." God's ways do not usually come naturally to us, but they are infinitely better than our ways.

We are in this together. Let's go forward with honesty and vulnerability—with God, with ourselves, and with others. Let's lock arms together spiritually, mentally, and emotionally against our common Enemy. Let's "consider how we may spur one another on toward love and good deeds" (Hebrews 10:24). Let's remember to climb up in the lap of our *Abba* Father, our "Daddy," and draw strength from His loving arms. Let's allow His love to flow freely through us to the people in our lives . . . especially our husbands. And let's take the time to share His love with the lost people that surround us.

Take Nothing for Granted

None of us knows how long we have to live on this earth. Only the Lord knows the number of our days. Nor do we know how many opportunities we will have to share our faith with others. For that reason, we need to make the most of each day and take advantage of every opportunity. God gave me a poignant example of this reality several years ago.

I had been meeting regularly with two different women whose husbands were emergency physicians in Ed's department. They were growing in their faith and so open and teachable—truly a delight to spend time with! One of the women had decided to host a breakfast at her home and invite the other wives whose husbands worked together. We had been praying together for these women.

On a beautiful fall morning, we met to enjoy breakfast together. Only Karen had accepted the invitation. But we had a sweet time together discussing our lives and the challenges of our husbands' schedules. God had worked in Karen's heart in an amazing way. During the course of breakfast, we brought up some issues relating to our faith and how that helped us to deal with difficulties in our lives. Karen asked several questions that had been buried in her tender heart. The other two women began to get quiet and pray for Karen. Since she was looking at me and asking me the questions, I prayed, too, that God would give me His answers.

Interestingly, Karen and I had a lot in common. We were the same age, had three birth children, and we both had husbands who were ER physicians. Our faith backgrounds, in our home of origin, were also very similar. God used that common ground, making our discussion open from the beginning. Karen and I had known each other for several years, which gave me the opportunity to share specifically about God and her need for a personal relationship with Him through the gift of Jesus' death and resurrection.

She knew I cared about her and was truly listening. I asked her if she wanted to pray with me to receive the gift of salvation. At the time, Karen chose to think about it some more, but said she really appreciated what I had to say and wanted to find a Bible she thought she might have at home and read some of the verses herself. I do not know what decision she made. I do know her heart was open and that she was seeking God.

Three days later, Ed got a call to come in to cover for one of his partners who had been in a serious accident. The secretary who made the call from the ER relayed terrible news. Someone had run a stop sign and crashed into the vehicle that Karen and her husband, Brad, were traveling in. Karen's parents, who were also in the car, were badly injured, but recovered. Brad was severely injured and in critical condition. Karen died. Yes, in one brief moment, this precious woman passed from this life to the next. She left behind a husband who never fully recovered, three children, extended family, and many friends. Everyone was shocked by the tragic news.

Though my first response was a flood of tears, immediately after that I was able to pray for this family. My first prayer was one of thanksgiving to God that He had allowed me the opportunity to talk with Karen about her eternal destiny. I would have had a hard time forgiving myself if God had provided that chance to share with her and I had not taken advantage of His purpose for that day. The Creator had given Karen and me a divine appointment. My hope and prayer is that Karen will be one of those people who greet me when I get to heaven!

Accept His Gift

I want to make sure you understand this free gift of salvation. Where are you in your relationship with God? Have you put Him on hold? Have you intimated to Him that you can't be bothered right now? After all, life is so busy, so overwhelming! You'll have plenty of time for Him later, right?

From the beginning of creation, God's plan has been for all men and women to be in an intimate relationship with Him. But that plan was initially rejected by Adam and Eve, as they intentionally went their own way, distancing themselves from their loving Father and Creator.

Sadly, in those foundational times, God's design was thwarted. Yet, a merciful plan of salvation was already in place, one that would invite all men and women back to restoration and intimacy. God's redemptive plan of action included Christ's death on the cross—as he took the punishment for all the sin and rebellion of mankind. Then Jesus rose from the grave—the ultimate demonstration of His victory over death and His power to bring promised fullness of life!

Have you made a personal decision to trust God? Have you admitted that, like everyone else, you have sin, you need forgiveness, and you have a deep-seated need for intimacy with your Creator? If you have not done this before, I pray you will stop right now and receive His indescribable gift. Jesus sacrificed His life so that you might live on this earth for Him and spend all of eternity with Him (see John 3:16). I truly hope you make this choice to live this life in light of eternity by making Jesus Lord of your life.

This is a gift freely offered to you by our extremely generous God. "For it is by grace you have been saved, through faith—and this not from yourselves, it is the gift of God—not by works, so that no one can boast" (Ephesians 2:8-9). Our part is to simply accept this gift that surpasses all others. This greatest gift meets our deepest needs. This gift miraculously transforms us like nothing else ever will.

Seek Him First

Now that I am in my fifties and have been married to Ed for more than thirty-six years, I can personally testify that I could not have made it through both the highs and lows of daily life without that personal relationship with my Savior. He has loved me like no other! He has empowered me, filled me with joy even in the hardest times, and given my life its truest purpose—to love God with all my heart, soul, strength, and mind, and to love others as myself! There is no greater plan for our lives than His.

You and I desperately need this God that the heavens declare. Our yearning hearts also confirm that divine diagnosis. Our husbands cannot and will not fulfill what only God is meant to satisfy in our lives. We must release our husbands from the burden of meeting all of our needs. Only God can truly meet our every need.

Will you commit to this in prayer? "Help me, O God, to focus on You, to allow You to change me and work in and through me . . . even in spite of me."

From the beginning of creation, His plan has been right in every way—in His created things, in created beings, and even in His carefully created relationships. "It is good," was a constant refrain from the start. The Bible says, "Take a good look at God's wonders. They'll take your breath away!" (Psalm 66:5 MSG).

My prayer is that as you focus on our Creator's loving plans in your own marriage, walking alongside other women who are facing the same challenges, you will grow closer to God, to your husbands, and to one another as you journey together.

Rx: Reflect daily on God's awesome creation as He reveals Himself to you, allowing you to know Him more intimately each day.

Chapter 2

℞ The Mind Matters

Name :

Age :

Address :

Date :

The law of the LORD is perfect, reviving the soul.

—Psalm 19:7a

Label ☐

Refill 0 1 2 3 4 5 PRN

I was meditating on this Scripture when I realized that the first promise mentioned in Psalm 19 is that the law of the Lord—God's Word—*revives* the soul. *Webster's* defines revive as "to restore to consciousness or life; to restore from a depressed, inactive, or unused state: bring back; to renew in the mind or memory."

Medical students learn early in their training the importance of properly assessing their patient. They examine basic life-sustaining systems to determine if the patient is well or if the patient is ill and in need of treatment. In the same way, as medical spouses, we need to periodically assess our own state of physical, mental, emotional, and spiritual health.

Are there any symptoms of system failure in your life? Have you recognized your desperate need for God and for the revival of your soul? He is the air we breathe. He is the Bread of Life. He is the water that quenches our thirst. Jesus said, "Everyone who drinks this water will be thirsty again, but whoever drinks the water I give them will never thirst. Indeed, the water I give them will become in them a spring of water welling up to eternal life" (John 4:13-14).

God heals our souls as He forgives, cleanses, restores, and guides us through His Word. Oh, how we need all that He offers to us when we begin to lag and drag, feeling alone! We need God's truth, His power, and the refreshment of the Spirit to revive us wherever we may find ourselves.

Renewing the Mind

I found this to be especially true during the first year of practice after residency. This time of transition can bring much stress for a new doctor and his spouse, especially if they are under the false impression that things will be better after residency. The truth is some things are better and some things are not! But I often failed to realize how important my thought process was during this time.

I remember one particularly challenging December when I was having a good, old-fashioned pity party. We were gearing up for the holidays, but we were living in Guam where Ed was serving time in the Navy for his medical-school scholarship. We only knew a handful of people, none of them very well. Our families were on the other side of the world. And at the time our girls were just two and four years old, which made the fact that Ed had duty on Christmas day even more difficult to endure.

I'd like to tell you I handled it well. Unfortunately, my thoughts continued to spiral downward as I mulled over all the negatives of our circumstances and how sorry I felt for myself. Of course, that was easy enough to do, but not helpful. Then one evening, when I was reading the story of the first Christmas to the girls, God spoke to my heart about His incredible gift of love to me. I realized it was time, long overdue, to celebrate this gift of Jesus!

As the days went by, God helped me to change my thinking by focusing on Him. We decided to do what we have done many times since—we simply changed the time we celebrated Christmas to a day when we could be together as a family. The girls and I were even invited to the home of another military family for Christmas Day. Several women were there whose husbands also had duty that day, along with their children. I still remember how special that time was and how God lovingly provided sweet "family" for me there. I realized that I had almost missed a wonderful blessing because I let my thoughts run unchecked instead of taking them "captive" as God urges us to do.

Keeping God's perspective in the midst of our disappointments and struggles can make all the difference. One lovely woman, married to a doctor for almost sixty years, recently shared a similar story with me. One Christmas several years ago, her family had special plans that were unexpectedly interrupted when her husband was called in for an emergent surgery. The entire family was disappointed when he had to leave for several hours to treat a ruptured appendix. However, in the days following the surgery, this wonderful doctor shared the Lord with his patient and she chose to follow Jesus. It wasn't long before she and her family began attending the doctor's church and she became a transformed woman who shared her faith with passion. The result was that her husband and most of their children also made the decision to follow Jesus.

Not long ago, the patient's husband was buried. As the doctor and his wife attended the funeral and saw the family gathered, with grandchildren and great-grandchildren everywhere, they couldn't help but ponder the ripple effect that had followed a simple act of obedience on one Christmas day. They were overwhelmed with thankfulness that God had allowed them to be part of His plan to change the course and destiny of an entire family. They realized that what seemed at the time like a great disappointment in ruined plans, from God's perspective was an even greater opportunity to affect an entire family for eternity.

We need to keep our minds saturated with God's truth and our thoughts focused on His perspective and not our own. Scripture tells us, "The good man brings good things out of the good stored up in his heart, and the evil man brings evil things out of the evil stored up in his heart. For the mouth speaks what the heart is full of" (Luke 6:45). Constantly storing up good things in our hearts, like God's Word, is what we need. We must "demolish arguments and every pretension that sets itself up against the knowledge of God, and we take captive every thought to make it obedient to Christ" (2 Corinthians 10:5). A healthy soul full of life is what I desire, not one that is shriveled up, lacking truth!

Just how do I do that? First, I must make myself aware of my thoughts. I have to think about what I am thinking about! You and I need to check often to see when our "stinking thinking" is leading us astray. An honest attitude check will quickly reveal this.

Recently, I was with a group of medical spouses as we discussed this very topic. We talked about the "recordings" that we tend to play over and over again in our minds. One woman confessed that her thoughts often descended to the point that she was convinced she did *everything* involved with the complexities of running a home while her husband wasn't doing *anything*. Another common refrain was, "Why is it *always* about his career—what about mine?"

Philippians 4:8 has a great remedy for this destructive thinking: "Whatever is true, whatever is noble, whatever is right, whatever is pure, whatever is lovely, whatever is admirable—if anything is excellent or praiseworthy—think about such things." These are powerful words that have the potential to change our thinking and, in turn, our lives.

What we are thinking comes out through our words and actions, so it is critical that we guard our thoughts. Try placing Philippians 4:8 in a conspicuous place where you will frequently see it. In our home, we have a bathroom cup, soap dispenser, and toothbrush holder that have this verse printed on them. It is very helpful for me to be reminded of what I should be thinking about as I meditate on this verse every morning and every night while brushing my teeth.

My attitude can slip so quickly to a place I do not want to go. My self-centeredness rears its ugly head—often when I least expect it. But Jesus' example always shows me a much better way. Because He loves us and wants the best for us, God will readily answer when we ask, "Lord, what thoughts need to be taken captive?"

Another very practical thing to do is to surround ourselves with friends who will encourage and uplift us. When we are around those who do not dwell on God's truth, we must be aware of their influence. Beware of women who complain about their husbands and are not seeking to build up their homes. Instead, do your best to show them God's way and the benefits that His way brings.

Who God Created You to Be

My pastor recently taught on a passage from John 18 about Jesus' arrest when Judas betrayed Him. Although the other disciples were with Him, the soldiers said it was Jesus they wanted. "Jesus answered, 'I told you that I am he. If you are looking for me, then let these men go" (v. 8). All of the disciples could easily have been arrested, but Jesus stood in the place of harm for these men. He would soon do this again for their sins and ours.

Jesus was totally surrendered to God's will. Every thought, every word, and every action was totally yielded to the Father. I sensed God was speaking to me about total surrender. Not that I could ever be perfectly surrendered to the Father's will like Jesus was, but I could imitate Him and yield more each day, with His power and with His help.

As I listened that day and continued to mull over this teaching, God began to bring to light different areas of self-centeredness in my life. He began to show me areas that I really didn't want to surrender to Him, unless I would get some kind of personal gain such as appreciation or recognition for what I had done. God reminded me that my life was to be wholly for Him and for His glory.

One clear winter day, He showed me a valuable lesson through His creation. I was watching a small sparrow as he sat on a branch near my window. As I was observing him, I caught a glimpse of another, larger bird flying high and some distance away. The white head and majestic spread of his wings convinced me that it was surely the bald eagle that we occasionally see flying near our home. I was distracted by the beauty of the eagle and forgot all about the sparrow until the eagle flew out of sight. It wasn't until later that day that God brought this observation of these two birds back to my mind.

For several days I had been struggling with living in the shadow of my husband. What he did was important and recognized with respect and admiration. When we were in a social setting and someone would ask what he did, the response of "ER physician" always got an admiring reaction. No one even asked what I did. Being co-directors in ministry didn't matter, because even though I knew I did at least half of the work, people would only mention Ed, as though only he did the ministry. You can certainly see how me-focused my thinking was.

The day I saw the birds was a particularly difficult one. That evening, I finally knelt down and cried out to the Lord. He met me in my need and reminded me how much He loves me and that

He sees all I do for Him. I was convicted of my desire to be noticed (at least equally!) and repented in tears for my wrong attitude and focus.

God then brought to my mind the birds I had observed earlier that day. He spoke to my soul, reminding me that He loved both of them. He had created each of them for His own purpose and pleasure. They were both content in being what He had created them to be. From my perspective, the eagle seemed more glorious, but God showed me a glimpse of His perspective and taught me a precious life lesson.

Yes, my husband might be seen as the eagle and get more attention, but that sparrow was equally loved by its Creator and was content resting in all that he had been made to be. It sang a joyful song as it perched on a branch outside my window, completely satisfied with life. Despite the cold and the difficulty of finding food in the frozen and snow-covered earth, he was only aware of doing what he had been created to do. It was a perfect picture of a life sweetly surrendered to the Father's will.

That is one of my deepest desires. I want to be all God has created me to be—content to live for His purpose and His glory only, to find my significance in Him alone. I long to be yielded to His will, to be the best I can be, entirely for Him.

Expectations and Resentment

On one particular weekend, I felt that it was particularly difficult to be the best I could be. A beautiful Saturday had dawned in the tropical paradise of Guam—a sacrifice, to be sure, but somebody has to go there! It was the kind of a sunny day that beckons you to pack up the kids and head to the beach. Visions of time spent digging in the sand with our three young children, frolicking in the sea, and enjoying a family picnic were delighting my mind.

That week, as a "single" parent, I had spent a lot of time with our three children, then ages 4, 2, and 2 months. You know the drill—hours at the hospital, the clinic, and on call had taken Ed away most of the week, and I felt that our family needed to spend quality time together. I also desperately needed a break and some help with the children. You may have noticed how many times "I" came up. That was a problem.

Another problem was that it had been such a busy week that there hadn't been time to talk about our expectations for the day—the *one* day that my husband finally had off. As the morning began, Ed announced to me that he had made plans to go scuba diving with a friend. The sudden realization that he had made other plans for the day hit me hard. Those plans did not include me or the children. I knew "I" was in trouble. My heart sank, and I instantly wanted to scream, *"No!"* followed by a list of all the reasons why he should not go. That sinking feeling progressed as I watched Ed begin to get his scuba-diving gear together. Clearly, we had formed our own plans without consulting each other.

Disappointment set in with a vengeance, the kind that is quickly followed by resentment. Then the dreaded pity party began. After all, hadn't I taken care of the children 24/7 for too many days in a row to count? Didn't I need adult conversation, too? Wasn't it perfectly fine to long for my husband to want to spend time with me and with our children?

I . . . I . . . I. In the midst of feeling the unfairness of the situation, a still small voice reminded me of my self-centeredness. The choice was truly mine. I wanted to justify my needs and remain angry and hurt. I wanted to insist that Ed not go. I wanted to demand that he go along with my plans.

Instead of venting on Ed, I turned to my heavenly Father. I asked Him for wisdom and grace in handling this situation. My husband did go scuba diving that day, and I had lots of time to think about how I would talk with him when he returned. Wow, how a battle raged within my sinful nature! But God prevailed and enabled me to let him go, then cheerfully greet him when he returned and, later, lovingly explain to him why this day was difficult for me.

This response, one I could only have managed with God's leading, reached my husband in a way that none of my confrontational "I" statements could have. Instead, we learned from this experience to discuss expectations in advance.

But the big takeaway lesson for me was a reminder that I was accountable to God alone for how I behaved. I couldn't blame my sinful reactions on the fact that someone else was "making" me sin. Most importantly, I was able to experience an incredible example of how reacting God's way brings peace and joy to my home in a way that can never happen if "I" is in control.

God continues to show me that I need to deal with my own issues (which are plentiful) and to get out of the way so He can deal with my husband's issues. I am only responsible to God for me. He is faithful in working in both of our lives to refine us.

Bob and Cheryl Moeller, authors and teachers, seem to heartily agree with God's lessons for me that weekend. In "Marriage Minutes," an online daily devotional, they write, "When we are trying to play the sculptor with our mate, it simply means we don't like the way our mate talks or behaves. We believe it is our calling to change him or her. So we constantly chisel away at our spouse, trying to make them more to our liking."

They continue, "There is a problem with playing the sculptor. Even if we are successful in changing our spouse . . . we now face a bigger problem than what we started with. We will now be married to someone who not only has their own set of problems, but ours as well. . . .

"We can't find anywhere in Scripture where we are commanded to change the person we are married to. . . . The only Person capable of changing the human heart is God Himself. So, if either of you has labored all these years to change each other (without success), we have good news for you—you're fired! . . . Your new job description . . . Accept your spouse just as they are, give thanks daily for the person God made them, and go to work full-time on repairing your own shortcomings!"

God enabled me to focus on Him, which in turn helped me to see Ed's need. He had been working really hard and needed a day to do something he enjoyed, so he had planned to scuba dive with a friend. Yes, maybe that decision was self-centered. If so, then it was between Ed and God. He needs to answer to God for that. I need to answer to God for only my words and actions.

The choice is mine, I realized, in handling the unfulfilled expectations and disappointments of life. I can live in frustration and succumb to choices that "suck the air" out of me (this I have done all too often!), or I can allow Him to use them to bring me closer to Him—allowing me to breathe in a way that restores and refreshes my body and soul.

A Heart Adjustment

I read a wonderful story written by Carol, an orthopedic surgeon's wife, in the Side by Side communication called On the Side. She does an inspiring job of explaining godly goals for our attitudes, that I want to share with you.

"Periodically, I have to sit down and adjust my way of thinking. I find that the direction of my thoughts directly impacts my attitude and therefore can directly affect the atmosphere in my home.

"Often, I set my mind on the way my husband's calling to be a doctor affects me and our children. I moan about the fact that he is not home for dinner every night. I complain that his pager gets so much attention. I whine about the time he spends studying rather than just being with me. The Bible is clear about the effect my behavior has on my husband and our home: 'A miserable heart means a miserable life; a cheerful heart fills the day with song,' (Proverbs 15:15 MSG).

"Something happened to me this summer that gave me the attitude adjustment I need to fill our days with song: My twelve-year-old son had major hip surgery. Benjamin's nine-hour surgery went very well. The x-rays looked perfect. But less than two days out of surgery, my boy went into respiratory distress that sent the staff running, my heart racing, and my sweet son to the Pediatric Intensive Care Unit. It was a horrible time, my friends. God's faithfulness was evident as His healing power touched Benjamin and turned him around faster than anyone expected. But the affect on me lingers.

"See, we are friends with our surgeon—he is Wade's partner, after all. Therefore, his wife and children are also our friends. So I knew we were interrupting family time when Dr. S. was paged to come running back to the hospital because my son was struggling to breathe on that Sunday afternoon. Just like I knew that his pager was interrupting mealtime when they paged him to check on giving Benjamin additional fluids. And I knew that his quality of family time was being affected when I saw the dark circles beneath his eyes when he checked on Benjamin the morning after he had been placed in the ICU.

"I knew. And yet, the relief I felt at having such a caring, time-giving surgeon far outweighed my concern for his sweet family. I was so thankful to have this doctor who was making sure every detail was getting the utmost attention to bring Benjamin back to his normal self. So thankful that this doctor was called to his profession and had a family who understands. I couldn't help but leave the hospital changed.

"Be assured that I am not perfect. I still want my husband home more than he is. I do. But today, when he is *not* home, I find myself praying for the family that he is ministering to—did their child just have surgery? Is the child in pain and is the mom scared to death? Are they anxious for a calming word from their doctor?

"Amazing, the affect this is having on my attitude toward Wade. I have been reminded that this is a calling. That he is ministering with every patient he encounters, and that my job is to ensure when he arrives home that he has a haven, a place where he can recharge and prepare for the next day.

"May I gently remind you, dear ones, that I am not unique? You can rest assured that whether you realize it or not, your husband and your children are being

41

affected by your attitude as well. But may I also remind you that God promises He notices every detail of our lives, and He promises that he will not let us down: 'God is not unjust; he will not forget your work and the love you have shown him as you have helped his people and continue to help them,' (Hebrews 6:10).

"God will not forget all you do to co-labor with your husbands. My prayer is that you will find rest in this promise as you strive to make your home a haven for your husband, thereby partnering in his work as a physician and helping him do his job to the best of his God-given abilities."

The Battle to NOT Lose My Mind

As a woman there are many battles I fight in this fallen world and in my daily life. However, the one for my mind seems to be the fiercest. My hands can be busy doing the right thing. My feet can carry me to the right spot. My face can even be smiling at the appropriate times. Yet it is deep down inside where God sees me on my own personal battlefield. In my mind I can still experience flashing swords, as attacks come on every side, leaving oozing wounds in my soul.

At times the attacks come in the form of destructive questions, as I've mentioned before. *Is this fair? Doesn't he notice what is going on with me? Does he think this is all about him? How can I possibly be expected to handle the demands of running our home without his help? How can we ever juggle both my career and his? Does anyone notice this is hard for me? God, are you still there?* Lies can also be used as effective ammunition by the Enemy. *You are all alone. No one sees you or understands or cares. This will never change. God has forgotten you!*

More than fifty years ago, Shirley Rice penned the following words addressing these same questions, lies, and moods. "When you are caught in the grip of a mood, go stand before the Lord, and like Elijah stay there, until the storm passes over and you hear the still small voice of God."

How do we stand before the Lord? There may be no better place to go than your prayer closet. You may be thinking as you read this, *Closet? I can't stop everything and go hide in a tiny, dark, little room. I just can't. You don't know my life!*

But Jesus encouraged us to get away from all of the distractions, whenever possible, in order to be revived and renewed. "But when you pray, go into your room, close the door and pray to your Father, who is unseen. Then your Father, who sees what is done in secret, will reward you" (Matthew 6:6).

What a model Suzanna Wesley was for us. She certainly knew how busy life could be. She had nineteen children, including the famous John and Charles, two men who rocked the Christian world with their passion for Christ. It has been written that she was known to put her apron up over her head to enter into a time of prayer. Her family knew this was a signal that Mom was praying and meant, "Do not disturb!"

The good news is that Jesus is always available to us in a quiet, Holy Spirit-filled spot; an inner calm, closet-like space. God is with us, tucked inside, offering counsel everywhere, in every moment. We can know that when we deliberately enter that place, God is there, always waiting and available. He will hold you. He will quietly speak truth. He will wield His sword on your behalf. He promises to empower you.

There are many ways to "take every thought captive" in our minds. One medical spouse tells of worshipping all day by having praise music playing in the background of her busy household, while driving in the car, maybe even while showering. How about tanking up your soul with His truth by listening to the music and Bible story CDs that are playing for your children's benefit? While not a typical "quiet time," it will touch you deeply if you let it, if you really have ears to hear.

You can do it! Whether you are all alone or in the middle of your busyness, just take the step. Open the door, wherever you are. He is there!

Be Transformed

Elizabeth George, in *Loving God with All Your Mind,* invites us to make these basic choices regarding our thoughts:

Work on what is real rather than worry about what is unreal.

Reach forward and press on rather than remaining a prisoner of the past.

Believe the truths of the Bible rather than trust emotions.

Act on what is revealed in Scripture rather than what appears to be.

This advice reminds us of how we need to make a conscious choice to love God with our minds. Our thinking directly affects our attitude and, in turn, our actions. It is crucial that we remind ourselves of this frequently. I sincerely invite you to make those same choices trusting that God has a good plan for you.

Romans 12:2 reminds us, "Do not conform to the pattern of this world, but be transformed by the renewing of your mind. Then you will be able to test and approve what God's will is—His good, pleasing, and perfect will."

God has good, pleasing, and perfect plans for us! We can be transformed people as we renew our minds, made new by His Word as we trust and obey Him. Take a moment and picture yourself squinting, looking out over the horizon, spying a needed oasis in the middle of a hot desert. Every road-weary, parched traveler cheers when the oasis comes into sight. Is that you? Are you really ready for His refreshment, for reviving? Are you aware of the thirst of your soul? His law is indeed perfect. May we run to the oasis of His truth! May your soul truly be revived as you spend time with Him.

Rx: Remember to do a daily attitude check and take every thought captive, making it obedient to Christ (2 Corinthians 10:5).

R

Chapter 3

In Pursuit of Wisdom

Name :

Age :

Address :

Date :

The statutes of the LORD are trustworthy, making wise the simple.

—Psalm 19:7b

Label ☐

Refill 0 1 2 3 4 5 PRN

Refill 0 1 2

Most of us are familiar with the legend—an unsuspecting person inadvertently rubs a shiny, magic lamp, and then a slow mist begins to emanate from the spout. Suddenly a powerful genie is released from captivity within and gratefully offers his stunned but delighted liberator the fulfillment of three wishes.

Have you ever imagined what you would ask for in that situation? Perhaps you would ask for money. Maybe you want to travel the world. Or you might wish for some luxury you have always wanted. Would you use your three wishes wisely or impulsively?

Thankfully, we don't need a genie. We have an all-knowing, all-powerful God who has an answer for every problem and provides for our every need. He is a generous God who invites us to boldly, yet humbly, bring Him the desires of our hearts.

If God said that you could have anything in the world, what would you choose? Solomon, the son of King David, faced this very decision when the Lord offered him whatever he desired (see 1 Kings 3:5). What did he ask for? Wisdom. I am in awe when I think of that choice. He could have asked for so many things, particularly for himself, but he asked for wisdom and discernment, that he might be a worthy king and ruler over God's people.

God was pleased with Solomon's choice and He wants to give us wisdom as well. The Bible says, "If any of you lacks wisdom, you should ask God, who gives generously to all without finding fault, and it will be given to you" (James 1:5).

God's Word shows us the foundation for wisdom, the value of wisdom, and the profit of wisdom. With that in mind, we come to the second benefit God reveals to us according to Psalm 19. He tells us that if we will put our full trust in His statutes, or His ways, we will be made wise.

Solomon wrote, "The fear of the LORD is the beginning of knowledge, but fools despise wisdom and instruction" (Proverbs 1:7). True wisdom begins with fearing and revering the Lord. The Lord is trustworthy. In other words, He is dependable, constant, honorable, faithful, and upright. He is worthy of our trust! His statutes and His established laws are for our good. We need to embrace His ways in all aspects of our lives because of who He is and how much He loves us.

Psalm 119:30-32 echoes the passionate desire of my heart: "I have chosen the way of truth; I have set my heart on your laws. I hold fast to your statutes, O LORD; do not let me be put to shame. I run in the path of your commands, for you have set my heart free."

Are you like me in your awe of God's glorious statutes? Is your heart zealous for His truth to become completely alive in you, to give you the wisdom you need to face each day? But I wonder if, like me, you sometimes fall short of trusting and obeying? The truth is we have all been there at one time or another. All have fallen short. All have gone astray. All come to Him sinful and simple.

But praise God, we are all invited to confess our sins, asking humbly for forgiveness. He invites us to then boldly come to His throne—waiting to learn, enjoying His love, gaining His wisdom.

Only our all-knowing Creator can show us how to navigate our ever-changing world!

Bloom Where You Are Planted

Change is difficult. Some people struggle with change more than others, but it's never easy. Just read the following synonyms for change out loud and try to keep your stomach from knotting up: shuffle, replace, swap, alter, modify, mutate, revolutionize, remodel, recast, reorganize, warp, bend, twist! I don't know anyone facing change that doesn't need wisdom from above.

From the very beginning, marriage brings with it lots of changes, many of which we are unprepared for. I learned this very early on in my marriage in a surprising way. For many years, I had a favorite pillow that I dearly loved despite its flat and tattered appearance. However, it became apparent after a few days of sleeping next to my new husband that there was a problem. His sneezing and watering eyes made it clear that he was allergic to my pillow.

The pillow had to go. So I made the first of millions of adjustments in my marriage. I chose to throw away this cozy and familiar place to rest my head and adapt to a new one. This is a minor example (although it did not feel like it at the time) of the many changes I would need to make. But dealing with these small issues helped me to cope with the bigger ones—like our major moves for Ed's residency and medical practice opportunities.

There was a time when cross-stitching was one of my preferred pastimes, and I stitched a piece with a flowered border surrounding words that read, "Bloom where you are planted." This framed phrase has hung in our bathroom for many years as we have moved from one home to another. It is a constant reminder to me that change will come and that I need to thrive wherever I am.

It's little wonder that the imagery of that saying grabs me. I really do enjoy gardening—both indoors and outdoors. Experience has taught me that some plants grow best in a certain type of light and with specific soil conditions. A perfect example occurred recently with one of my more reliable indoor plants. The tall tropical palm seemed as though it was doing well in the study, but due to some space issues, it got moved to the living room. It quickly began to grow, and I realized that it looked much healthier. The funny thing is I would never have known its potential had it not been transported to an area with slightly different lighting.

Sometimes we aren't even aware of our own needs or potential. God alone is the perfect Gardener. He knows the requirements of each of His "plants." If I am in a location where I am not thriving well, it is very likely that I need more "light from the Son" and the nourishing soil of the Word. I need the "Living Water" to flow in me and through me. I am always amazed how quickly this brings about new growth in my life.

It's All In the Attitude

Have you ever noticed that the woman is the one who sets the emotional climate in her home? Our attitude makes a huge difference to our families. Yes, it is convicting, but so true. If I notice others around me are grumpy and complaining, then I need to look at myself to see if the "wilting" has started with me. But the good news is we can also be a contagiously cheerful influence when our attitude is "blooming."

Sometimes it is difficult to grow and bloom where God places us. Often, this is because we forget that it is our loving heavenly

Father who has "planted" us. He knows where the soil conditions are just right. Even if our circumstances seem particularly challenging, the truth is that every place has its advantages and disadvantages. I'm just so glad that God knows about every important detail of our lives—even before they happen!

Our first move to Jacksonville, Florida, for Ed's residency seemed to be an easy one. I was ready for the adventure and, admittedly, quite naïve about what a major move meant. I left my dear family, great friends, a familiar home, and a wonderful job I loved as a pediatric nurse. I arrived in Florida eight months pregnant, with the pressing need of finding a doctor and the daunting task of unpacking and setting up a home by myself. To add to that, I didn't know a single person and was completely clueless about the repercussions of my husband's schedule and the fact that he would rarely be home during that internship year.

But God knew exactly what I needed. He brought a special group of medical wives into my life that helped and cared for me and told me about God's love for me. They explained what my soul had been searching for—a personal relationship with God through His gift of Jesus. They lived out Scripture and taught me how to study the Bible. God transplanted me and provided abundantly beyond what I even knew I needed!

The moves that followed came whether I was ready for them or not. Each one seemed harder than the last, as it always meant leaving more dear friends and familiar surroundings. Reminding myself of His provision during that first move and that God was the One "planting" us made all the difference.

Moving was inevitable during the years of my husband's school, residency, and practice. But a bad attitude was optional. I could choose to be positive and see the good in the change, or I could choose to be negative and dwell on the bad. The choice to see the positive made all the difference for me and for those around me!

The Place of Blessing

Have you ever noticed that the two heroes of faith who get the most press are Abraham and Moses? A quick review of their lives reveals that they experienced many moves and changes in their walks with God.

In Genesis 12:1 God gave Abraham his marching orders and said, "Go from your country, your people and your father's household to the land I will show you." Stop and think about what that really meant for Abraham and Sarah, Abraham's wife. They had to leave their country, home, and beloved families behind. Imagine the tears and the fears of the unknown. You can relate, can't you?

Interestingly, the next two verses are filled with God's promises of blessing after blessing. In fact, throughout the rest of the book of Genesis, God repeatedly declares His blessing over Abraham and all of the generations that would follow, including you and me. The promise of a Savior for the world is woven into this promise to Abraham.

As a little baby, Moses was passed multiple times from home to home and then from country to country. Was he afraid? He must have been. Did he obey? Most of the time he did. Did he ever feel alone? Surely he must have. Was God faithful? Always!

The God of Abraham and Moses—and for that matter, the God of Ruth and Esther and Mary, Jesus' mother—is your God too. He knows the way. Just like each person whose story is told in His Book, He has a great plan for you. Jeremiah 29:11 states, "'For I know the plans I have for you,' declares the LORD, 'plans to prosper you and not to harm you, plans to give you hope and a future.'" His promises are true, dear one. His love is perfect. He knows best where you and I will thrive—in soil that He cultivates and an environment where He will nurture us. This is where His blessing awaits!

Staying Connected

Adjusting to life's many changes can lead to a problem of focusing too much on self. It is never hard to see how things affect us personally and to concentrate on how *we* must cope. But if I choose instead to look at how these changes affect my spouse, it enables me to see the world from his perspective. It requires a purposeful mind-set of trying to understand and support him through everything that comes.

Have you ever heard the phrase, "Walk a mile in my shoes?" Seeing the world through your husband's eyes, or imagining your toes slipped down into his thick-soled shoes, makes a huge difference. If you do not take the time and make the effort to connect with one another, you may soon find that you are busy living in two separate worlds.

Many times it seemed as though Ed and I were spinning in our own separate orbits. I really struggled with this. I wanted to be a part of his world and have him be a part of mine. This truly is a godly desire, set in place by God as two individuals are mysteriously made one through the covenant of marriage.

Connecting during residency definitely required some creativity! I thought it would be helpful to have more time with my other half. Since there were few ways to make this happen, my options were limited. I decided that I would take dinner to Ed at least once a week when he was on call at the hospital. There were times I said to myself, "What were you thinking?" when I realized all the work it took to plan, prepare, and carry dinner to him. (Takeout was fine on occasion too, but I wanted him to have some home-cooked food made with love!) With the added responsibility of having a child or two in tow, I did sometimes wonder if an "I Love You" card would have sufficed!

Let me take a moment to warn those of you who are optimists like me. (Of course, if you are a bit of a pessimist, you are probably snickering under your breath at this very moment!) If you decide to take dinner to your husband, be prepared to wait because he will not be ready when he says he "thinks" he will be ready. Then, he will likely eat very fast. (Ed developed this habit during residency when he knew he would have little time to eat. Despite nearly inhaling his food, he lost twenty pounds during those years, so he clearly did not eat often enough!) And, perhaps most disappointing of all, he will be called away much too soon.

However, all of your effort is not in vain! You have spent time with each other, you have communicated your love for him in a tangible way, and you have had a chance to see his world. You may even have a chance to kiss him and tell him you love him. Hopefully he kisses you back and says, "I love you" and "Thank you so much for coming." But, realistically, he may mumble something about the next patient he needs to see and though he may *think* all of these things, he may not say them. This is a great time to extend grace to him and remember that God sees all we do in His name to minister to others.

It might seem foolish that I spent so much time and energy looking for ways to connect with my husband. But I realized how truly important those visits were one evening when I informed our daughter, Kristi, that we were taking dinner to Daddy at the hospital. She excitedly exclaimed, "We are going to Daddy's house!"

"Oh, no honey," I replied. "Daddy works at the hospital, but he lives at our house."

"No," Kristi insisted with two-year-old determination, "he lives at the hospital." It broke my heart that I could not convince her that he did in fact live at our home and not at the hospital. I could agree with her assessment however, because that is often where she saw him. He was home after she went to bed, gone before she was up, or away from home completely for a day or two. So, she would naturally assume that he lived in that "big, gray house."

My husband and I did have many discussions about how to be more involved in each other's lives. I really felt like Ed understood the concept of sharing our worlds when he surprised me one day and called me from the emergency room. It was a very brief call and all he said was, "Please pray for me. I really feel like I am drowning with all the really sick people I need to see and one really bad case. I am struggling with having a good attitude."

That was it. Short. Simple. Yet, to me, it was huge! He was asking me to be a part of his world. He was sharing his struggle. He needed me. He wanted me to pray for him. Wow. I have often received those calls over the years, and I still treasure the privilege that I have been given to bring my husband's request to the throne of our heavenly Father. In those moments we are connected in the best of all ways—spiritually.

Sharing our needs, our dreams, and our struggles allows us to be a part of one another's lives. The Bible reminds us that, "Two people are better off than one, for they can help each other succeed. If one person falls, the other can reach out and help. But someone who falls alone is in real trouble. Likewise, two people lying close together can keep each other warm. But how can one be warm alone? A person standing alone can be attacked and defeated, but two can stand back-to-back and conquer. Three are even better, for a triple-braided cord is not easily broken" (Ecclesiastes 4:9-12 NLT). Just picture that—you and your husband connected and wound up together with our powerful God. That, my friends, is a strong cord!

The "Aroma" at Home

A healthy connection with one another leads you to want to be together more. When I am supportive and make an effort to listen to my husband and to understand his world, it causes him to *want* to come home and enjoy the sweetness of being together. I long to be home with him, too. That means I need to guard against tension between us that can give our home a "sour" smell.

Favorite fragrances and aromas awaken our senses and cause us to take notice. In our house, the familiar smells of brownies baking, fresh coffee brewing, and scented candles burning draws us in and makes us feel at home. What are your favorites? In 2 Corinthians 2:14-16 Paul writes, "But thanks be to God, who always leads us as captives in Christ's triumphal procession and uses us to spread the aroma of the knowledge of him everywhere. For we are to God the pleasing aroma of Christ among those who are being saved and those who are perishing. To the one we are an aroma that brings death; to the other, an aroma that brings life."

Wow! God, through Christ, uses us to draw people to Him by using our "fragrance"—our appeal. How convicting to think of the importance of our lives having pleasing qualities that in word and action will draw others to Christ—that will point them to a saving knowledge of Him. Our "fragrance" should encourage believers and draw unbelievers to come to know and love God.

Unfortunately, one of the most difficult places to exude this wonderful scent is in our own homes. It is the place where we let down our guard. We like to say that, "We let it all hang out!" We forget to treat others around us as we wish to be treated ourselves. We often let the "garbage" linger too long and it begins to reek.

When our husbands are often gone, it is easy to fall into a habit of complaining. Cheryl, a dear friend and wife of a busy gastroenterologist, purposely made it a point to never complain about her husband's being on call or working. She made up her mind to not complain by reminding herself whenever necessary that he was "working for the patients' best and to provide for our family." This has made a big difference to her husband (and her marriage) over the years. How wonderful that with godly discernment she has chosen to not be "the quarrelsome wife" who drives her husband into living "on a corner of the roof" (see Proverbs 21:9).

Most of the time we can convince ourselves of the significance of our spouse being gone. However, it is much more difficult when we have our hopes set on him being available for certain events or special occasions—only to get the familiar, dreaded calls. The first call comes when he is already late, saying that he is trying to get home. The second call lets us know there is no chance he will make it home in time. When a special date is canceled or he misses your child's birthday party, it is hard to not be discouraged—or even angry.

Take those frustrations to the Lord and pour out your heart to Him. Try to see your husband's perspective. I would often need to remind myself that Ed really did want to be home and that he was just as disappointed as I was. On top of that, he had to deal with the guilt that he had missed yet another opportunity to be there for his family.

We can also grow in wisdom in helping our children deal with the inevitable disappointments that will come. We could tell them that daddy has let them down. We can complain that he is once again missing an important occasion instead of making it a priority to be there. Or we can choose to be a sweet fragrance that builds our children's relationship with their father by explaining how much he wanted to be there and how sad and sorry he is to be missing their special event. Reassure them that daddy loves them very much and will participate in some other way to celebrate their moment.

In these moments, remember that how you react not only sets the tone for the rest of your family, but also leaves an aroma—good or bad—in your home. Greet your husband with a hug and kiss and tell him you are glad he is home. Remind him that he is not a failure at being a good husband and father—for he is likely feeling this way. Prepare for an amazing response and a recharge in your relationship connection!

Recently I was sitting next to a resident's wife at a wedding reception, and we discussed how she and her husband have been coping with the stresses of residency. She shared that one of the hardest things for her was not how much her busy husband was gone. Instead, the greatest struggle came when he did finally arrive home, only to be so exhausted that he would fall asleep. Knowing he was in the house but was not available to spend time together was really hard.

Other wives have shared with me over the years that they resent the time their husbands spend on the computer, watching TV, or playing video games. Trying to understand his need to "decompress" after a stressful day may help you to give him grace. He is moving from a place of "life and death" to home and may need some time to mentally adjust. You need time to adjust, too. When you are both ready, talking about mutual goals for your marriage may help you both use the time you do have together wisely. I know of several couples who have simply put their TV in a closet so as not to be tempted to have that "eat up" the limited time they do have together.

It has been said that the woman in the home is the invisible builder. You don't necessarily notice the foundation she is laying, but everyone in the home is well aware of the effects. "The wise woman builds her house, but with her own hands the foolish one tears hers down" (Proverbs 14:1). The wise woman looks for opportunities to positively reinforce the foundation of healthy relationships. She refrains from tearing down the very home she desires to build. She looks for opportunities to spread the fragrance of Christ in her home and in her areas of influence.

Taming the Tongue

When was the last time you tried to put something together without following the directions? Not long ago I made a loaf of bread in my breadmaker. I should say I *tried* to make a loaf of bread. Unfortunately, the small blade that mixes the dough was not properly attached and an hour later the ingredients were still sitting there unmixed. Forgetting to check the small kneading blade had ruined the loaf of bread.

The manufacturer had outlined the directions I needed to follow, but I didn't bother to check them and had left out an important step. In the same way, our Creator also has directions for us. Most of them are pretty simple . . . at least to understand. It's the "following them" part that usually gets us into trouble. I often think I know what I am doing, but He alone knows what is best for me.

Much like that little blade in my breadmaker, the small tongue inside my mouth has the potential to ruin a lot more than bread if I don't use it as God directs. The Bible says, "The tongue is a small part of the body, but it makes great boasts. Consider what a great forest is set on fire by a small spark" (James 3:5). Even such a small part of us can cause *big* problems if not run according to the directions—God's statutes.

So what should we do? The Bible gives us wise advice, saying, "Everyone should be quick to listen, slow to speak and slow to become angry" (James 1:19). When we feel offended or neglected, it is so easy to say harsh words and vent our anger. So much damage can be done before we even begin to think about the consequences. That is why God reminds us to do the opposite of what comes naturally. The Message puts it this way, "Lead with your ears, follow up with your tongue, and let anger straggle along in the rear." God is ready and willing, through His Word, to lead us on a much wiser path!

Perhaps there is nothing quite as important as watching what comes out of our mouths. A whole book could be written on this subject alone. But most of us, myself included, don't need more information. We need more yielding to the Holy Spirit's leading. We need more application of what we already know God's Word says. We don't need more guilt from the damage done by our words.

Instead we need to more deeply grasp God's incredible love for us. Then we will want to bless others around us as His love flows through us and out of our mouths. If we could just remember to be quick to listen and slow to speak or become angry, we would eliminate most of what we later need to ask forgiveness for. "Do not merely listen to the word, and so deceive yourselves. Do what it says" (James 1:22).

Taming the tongue is simply a must for a wise woman. Otherwise, it is like what happens if a tube of toothpaste is tightly squeezed, letting its contents ooze out. It is simply impossible to get that toothpaste back into the tube. In the same way, it is impossible to take back words that we have spewed out of our mouths.

Don't you wish sometimes that our mouths functioned like a computer? Wouldn't it be great if I could delete what I spoke without thinking or erase unkind words when I see how they hurt my husband, my child, or my friend? If only I could go back and rearrange things so as not to miscommunicate. If only I could read what I am going to say before I hit "send" so that I could change the words that were not edifying.

Psalm 139:4 tells us, "Before a word is on my tongue, you know it completely, O LORD." I am awed to know that God knows the words I will say before I even say them. How I need to be listening to His still small voice to stop me before the "sparks" fly! Before my "harsh word stirs up anger" (Proverbs 15:1).

Whether we are adapting to times of change, struggling to find precious time to connect with our husbands, or striving to bring sweet fragrance to our home in our daily words and deeds, may the Lord of all help us to obey His great statutes of wisdom. May we allow His love and His Word to transform us from simple to wise each and every day!

Rx: To banish an unpleasant aroma in your heart and life, practice the following four capsules of wisdom daily: Bloom where you are planted, watch your attitude, stay connected, and guard your tongue.

R

Chapter 4

Maximize the Moment

Name :

Age :

Address :

Date :

The precepts of the LORD are right, giving joy to the heart.

—Psalm 19:8a

Label ☐

Refill 0 1 2 3 4 5 PRN

My husband loves maps. Whenever someone mentions visiting a new or exciting place in the world, he can hardly contain himself until he finds its location in our atlas. Even in this age of GPS, satellite imagery, and easy Internet mapping services, he still prefers using his well-worn paper maps. For him, these maps represent the cumulative wisdom and experience of travelers who have made countless journeys in the past and recorded their findings in the form of pictures and symbols for those that would follow after them.

Whether you prefer technology or paper, we all need maps to help us find our way. *The Message* translation of Psalm 19:8 tells us, "The life-maps of God are right, showing the way to joy." Embracing God's Word by following His principles gives us heartfelt joy. This inner delight comes when we love God with all of our being and confidently follow His Word, because we know God's instructions are right and just.

The word "right" in this verse points to a way that is not crooked or twisted, but instead follows a path of moral good, fitness, and even innocence—the straight and, sometimes, the narrow. True joy comes from a life focused on God's purity and holiness, rather than on the circumstances and brokenness of the world around us.

What direction is your life heading right now? Is your heart filled with gladness and peace, or are you lacking His joy deep inside? The culture in which we live would suggest that the only way to happiness is through self-indulgence and the pursuit of worldly pleasure, but the Bible tells us differently: "You make known to me the path of life; you will fill me with joy in your presence, with eternal pleasures at your right hand" (Psalm 16:11).

To what or whom are you listening? What reading material in your house is most dog-eared? How dusty is your Bible? What is the compass of your life? Only when we spend time with the Lord, study His Word, and follow His direction can we experience joy in the midst of life's challenges and demands.

Free from Expectations

When Ed was applying to medical school, someone shared with me the "proper" etiquette of being a doctor's wife. She told me that she had been a doctor's wife since the "old days," when a wife was expected to attend certain social events, be involved in particular activities, wear white gloves, and be dressed in the latest fashions—as she set the standard for style in the community. Oh, my! I am so thankful that my confidence comes from God's guidelines and not hers. I am so glad that silly "white glove" business has changed, aren't you?

Of course, both fashion trends and cultural norms change constantly. But for wives in the medical community, many other things do not. Certain stereotypes and assumptions are still much the same. A doctor's wife is often seen as rich and spoiled. She has no problems, no pressures, no challenges. Her life is a walk on easy street. Most people do not realize the huge personal debt acquired from years of expensive medical schooling. They are unaware of the personal sacrifices required. Few understand the loneliness.

I came across a delightful book by Elizabeth Prentiss, *Stepping Heavenward,* that was published in 1869. This insightful story describes the life of a woman married to a doctor, and the following excerpt is an example of what has not changed even 140 years later:

> Our honeymoon ends today. There hasn't been quite as much honey in it as I expected. I supposed that Ernest would be at home every evening, at least, and that he would read aloud, and have me play and sing, and that we would have delightful times together. But now that he has got me he seems satisfied and goes about his business as if he had been married a hundred years. In the morning he goes off to see his list of patients; he is going in and out all day; after dinner we sit down to have a nice talk together, the doorbell invariably rings, and he is called away. Then in the evening he goes and sits in his office and studies; I don't mean every minute, but he certainly spends hours there.

Yes, the times have changed, but many of the struggles we face are very much the same. No one needs to convince a medical spouse of the reality of sacrifice, especially in the area of spending time together. It begins in medical school when you try to plan *limited* social activities around his exam schedule. It continues in residency when you realize you must either choose to spend all of your time alone or attend functions by yourself. The "establishing in practice" years bring new adjustments as you move, set up house mostly by yourself, and help your family begin life in your new community. Over time, we become quite independent and do many, many things on our own. That is just what we do as wives of physicians.

But in the same way that those on the outside can have unrealistic views of who we are, we too can be lured into believing that we can do it all. That is a lie. To live by God's truth and experience joy every day, we must let go of unrealistic expectations of ourselves. You are only supposed to do what God is calling you to do. That means carefully and prayerfully evaluating what you commit to. Don't say "yes" to something until you are sure you have a "yes" from God. Follow only God's "life-maps." Taking the wrong road—yours instead of His—even though it may seem to make sense at the time, can send you wandering off into the distant land of despair.

A Balancing Act

A friend of mine once suggested good, practical advice—that in order to avoid overload in my life, I should not say "yes" to anything unless I was prepared to say "no" to something I was already doing. Remember, as the spouse of an often-absent husband, you may need to do some things that you would prefer not to, things that your husband simply does not have time to handle.

You may also find it tempting to over-commit and fill up your schedule when your busy husband is away for many hours (sometimes days), and then find it hard to adjust when he does reappear. It is so important to clearly communicate our expectations with our husbands. Neither of you want to be laboring in vain. Hours are too precious. Psalm 127:1 clearly proclaims, "Unless the LORD builds the house, its builders labor in vain." You are builders together.

One idea that worked well for Ed and I was to commit to spend some time together on Sunday evenings each week to talk about our week and pray together. (Of course, we needed to be flexible with our schedules and occasionally moved it to another night.) This became a treasured time for me as we came together before God. It helped us better understand each other's plans and expectations. I truly heard what was on Ed's heart when he prayed. This helped me to know more specifically how to pray for him during the week.

I remember that our pastor during Ed's years of residency had suggested that all couples should get away alone for a weekend every six months. This is wise advice, though not always practical. But despite the time obstacle, make every effort to plan some regular time to enjoy being together and to assess goals that are important to you as individuals and as a couple. If this priority is not addressed in a timely way, frustrations and misunderstandings can build up, much like the picture of a dam when a river is at flood stage, water sloshing over the top, just ready to burst. And it can burst out wildly at times!

One seasoned doctor's wife, Heather, shares how she and her husband handled the challenges of their overloaded life together in a very courageous way:

> I think the best part of life as the spouse of a doctor is that so many people love and appreciate my husband for the kindness he's shown to them. I've often had people extend their love to me just because they learn that I'm married to the doctor who was so good to them or their loved ones. That is a really addictive feeling to both my husband and me. But it can become a problem when we don't put proper boundaries in place. The need for

that appreciation can sometimes cause the vocation of physician to seem like a hungry ogre that's never satisfied.

My husband and I experienced a lot of stress in our marriage in his early years of practice because of that drive for appreciation. As our family grew, I needed more of my husband's time and was disappointed daily by the amount of time he had to spend at work. He found it difficult to come home to a house full of needs when he'd spent so much time at work. It became a very destructive cycle in our marriage.

If you want to have a successful marriage in a medical family, you must learn to put the job in its place. It is not to master your family. You must master it. There will always be more work to do in any job. A great marriage and family life must be prioritized. We ended up leaving the practice that was coming between the two of us and started over in a place where the schedule would be more family friendly. Since then we have guarded our commitments so that we can have a more balanced life.

I encourage every wife to read about godly boundaries. There are several good books on that subject. As my understanding of God and His ways have grown, I've been able to balance the rest of my life better. Life is full of successes and failures. Learn from both of them and don't get discouraged. It's true that when we seek God first, He'll add unto us everything that we need.

Just as Heather and her husband seemed to have experienced, I have watched friends take on too many commitments or have their children involved in far too many activities. I have been there myself and learned that it is better to think things through before the frenzy sets in.

One evening, our oldest daughter had a field hockey game at the high school, our second daughter had a horseback-riding lesson outside of town, and our three sons each had soccer practice on three different fields. Whew! Lots of stress as I tried to get them each where they needed to be with the right equipment and feed them dinner out of a slow cooker in our minivan. Needless to say, friends were a true lifesaver that night as my husband was busy saving lives at the ER and couldn't share in the craziness.

Realizing the importance of thinking through our family schedule was a valuable lesson for us. Our family learned to pray about what activities God wanted us to be involved in. There are so many choices of good things to participate in. Choose wisely and avoid the trap of being too busy to do the best things—like just enjoying time together!

Some couples benefit from limiting electronics. For us, the decision to eliminate TV watching, except on rare occasions, has been one of the best time-management decisions we have made. We found it to be so much more beneficial to spend time with God and in building relationships with others. This is time that matters for eternity.

Talking about goals ahead of time really helps. We learned to schedule things on our calendar that were priorities to us, like time with God, date time as a couple, and quality time with our children (both one-on-one and all together), as well as time with our friends. That way we weren't left trying to find some way to "squeeze in" what we most desired to spend our time on.

Live in the Moment

We can get so busy that we don't stop to think about how we spend our time. Do you find yourself constantly running around? Is your daily calendar so full that there is no room for "divine appointments" in your day? When we have every minute planned, we are unlikely to respond to God's agenda for our day. Sadly, there have been times that I have missed these opportunities and truly regretted making my agenda more important than God's. We often miss the blessings God has for us when we are focused on our own busyness instead of Him.

God has graciously given each of us the gift of twenty-four hours in each day. That translates to exactly 1440 minutes per day to use as we desire. He does not force us to use them His way—that is our choice. Do you see each day as a gift from Him to be used for Him? It certainly changes my perspective on the way I use my time when I view it this way. I am at long last learning to leave pockets of time available for the many unexpected opportunities that arise.

In *A Minute of Margin,* Richard Swenson, MD, writes, "Busyness is not a synonym for kingdom work: it is only busyness. And busyness is sometimes what happens to us when we forget who God is. Busyness displaces the power of the present moment. The present moment is infinitely small, yet God resides there. When we hurry, we look beyond the present, and in so doing, miss it entirely. We are aiming for something in the future, but not in the moment.

"Christ, however, lived and ministered in the moment. He accepted daily ministry opportunity as it came in the person standing before Him. . . .We must be willing to have Christ-like criteria with which to judge our choices and then be willing to actually use these criteria as a guide for daily living."

A perfect example of making the most of opportunities is found in Luke 8:40-48. Jesus was on His way to heal Jairus' dying daughter, after being begged to do so by her grieving father. This was important work, yet Jesus stopped abruptly to minister to a woman who had been bleeding for twelve years. Jesus knew power had gone out from him when she touched his garment. The crowds were pressing against Him, and He was in a hurry. He could have simply continued on His way to heal the dying girl, yet He recognized the faith of the woman and stopped to meet her need and give her God's peace.

Letting go of the pressure to do what others expect you to do is necessary for your health—mentally, physically, emotionally, and spiritually—and frees you up to be who God created you to be. We need to use Jesus' example as our map for the days in which we live. Our husbands really need these precepts, too, in the busyness of their hectic lives. Isn't it interesting to note that Moses, one of the most capable, well-trained leaders of the entire Bible, was directed in Exodus 18 with the same kind of wisdom? One person trying to do too much only served to lessen his effectiveness, not to mention his quality of life!

Romans 12:2 directs us to "not conform to the pattern of this world." Instead, we are to renew our minds, leading us to God's righteous will. There is no doubt about it, the world around us, hand in hand with the Enemy, is indeed trying to conform us to its way of thinking. What are the expectations of the world that influence your thinking? How do they compare to the truth of God's Word?

Psalm 19:8a says, "The precepts of the LORD are right, giving joy to the heart." *Precept* is defined as, "a rule or principle imposing a particular standard of action or conduct." God tell us that His rules are right and bring us joy. How easy it is to fall into the frenzy and fatigue trap of our world. We must be on guard, believing God is the One whom we can trust, the One who always works on our behalf!

Time to Talk

How freeing it is to wisely discern the activities God wants us to be involved in and stick to only those. Life can be chaotic enough in a busy medical marriage without feeling the pressure to be doing all that others expect you to do. You need to allow time for your priorities . . . including communicating with one another. We all know this to be true, but at times it is so difficult to follow through on what is most important to us.

Recently, an e-mail appeared in my inbox. It was sent by a resident's wife that I have mentored for some time. She described this common struggle well in her note: "So much time apart leaves little time to work on your marriage. Sometimes I feel as though Ray and I are running into the same brick wall because we don't have the time or emotional energy to break it down right now. I've been talking with a counselor who has advised me that for the foreseeable future this might not be a good time to talk with him about some things. This may be a season where I just continue to extend grace. And I can see where he's coming from. If I bring something up to Ray that I foresee as a problem, he gets very overwhelmed. He feels as though he can't stay on top of his job and to think he's not staying "ahead" in his marriage is too much for him to handle. I was wondering what you thought. And as always, wondering if you might pray for us."

This dear friend understands the difficulty of balancing what *really* needs to be discussed, with learning when she just needs to let go. It's hard to "ruin" the first two hours of uninterrupted time with your husband in ten long days with a difficult discussion of how you are hurt or struggling or how the marriage is not going so well.

The lack of time to talk was most difficult for me after those times when conflict would surface in our relationship. As women, we want to have the disagreement resolved and the connection restored. We long for things to be made right again. Since we tend to mull over the issue, our thoughts and emotions remain unsettled until we can work through the problem. God has wired men to be able to focus on what they are doing at the time and let other areas be temporarily out of their thoughts. So, while we are agonizing over the tension in the relationship, they are oblivious to it for the time being.

Those are the moments we really need to run to God and pour out our hearts and tears to Him. This will allow us to much more constructively and lovingly communicate when the time is finally right. God mightily uses the waiting time, if we allow Him to. Oh, the sweet bliss of a reconciled relationship with our husband!

Sarah, a former member of Side by Side in another city, joined our Richmond group when her husband started his residency. During this time, she found herself learning to rejoice, even in the challenges, as she ran to the Lord for wisdom in keeping her marriage pleasing to Him. The lessons she learned about finding "joy even in the trials" are reflected in her advice to other residents' wives:

> When the excitement of graduation and moving faded, reality set in fast.
>
> Reality is that a medical resident is never home. He or she will spend more hours at the hospital than there are hours in the day. As a medical wife I had to get used

to my husband being gone all the time. I had to get used to taking care of everything at the house as if I were a single person. I had to get over my resentfulness of the hospital and the patients that I felt were taking my husband away from me.

It is hard when you feel as though you are not on the top of your husband's priority list. There were times when I did not see my husband for days because he got home after I went to bed and left before I woke up, if he came home at all. We had many minor squabbles for months. I resented having this beautiful new house to clean, do repairs on, and pay bills for, yet never got to enjoy. I resented having to remind my husband to call his mom, get a haircut, and sometimes even to get gas for his car.

Find new ways to communicate with your husband. Texting is great because it usually works in the hospital. Make sure you have your husband's pager number and do not give it out to friends and family members. Write notes and leave them in his pocket or on the bathroom mirror with a dry erase marker. We also have a little game going. I hide a blue stuffed bunny for him, and he hides a pink one for me. When we find our bunny we call the other and tell them where we found it and set it on the bed to be hidden again. Sometimes it takes months for me to find my bunny, but it always makes me smile. A good marriage is in the details, the tiny things you do for each other.

We also have another factor to consider besides extremely limited time together, which is that he is

I disagree! ~~

constantly dealing with people in crisis situations. Remember, if your life and limb are not in danger, your husband may not think your issue is such a big deal. Add exhaustion to this . . . likely for both of you . . . and it is a recipe for disaster.

Doctors deal with life and death every day. Working in a hospital is a serious place. There is no such thing as casual Friday or let's go to lunch for so-and-so's birthday. There is no chit-chatting around the water cooler. It is a high-stress, high-stakes, hard-knocks environment.

My husband would get home and if it wasn't time for bed he would literally veg out. Sometimes I felt ignored like I was the housekeeper. Realize that he does love you (or he would not have come home) but he is mentally and physically exhausted.

Do not plan a surprise date night. He needs time to relax and decompress before he can shift from doctor to husband. Do not let him ignore and neglect your relationship either. Let him know you need to hear that he loves you. Yes, he has a demanding job and will for the next fifty plus years, so work *now* on ways to redefine your marriage before you grow apart or have "irreconcilable differences."

Find ways to share feelings when you are not upset or angry. Do not be a drama queen every time you get to talk to your husband. The time you actually have together is precious, so if you are angry about something, write a note or send an e-mail. If it is not resolved that way, find a time when you are calm and he is not exhausted to work it out.

Through all of these valleys, my loneliness pushed me closer to my best friend, Jesus. He helped me see the light at the end of the tunnel. Jesus helped me find a new perspective. My husband was not choosing to be away from me, he was fulfilling God's call on his life. And when my husband does come to the house, it needs to be a safe place . . . a home rather than a place where his nagging wife has a to-do list for him.

Molly, an energetic physician married to another physician, and also a busy mother of four, can certainly give insights in many areas. She shared a story that really illustrates the importance of seeking the Lord's wisdom in how to communicate with each other.

You cannot imagine the stress your spouse is carrying around from day to day—they can sometimes be so used to it they don't even realize they are near the breaking point. Of course, not all days are like that, but they seem to come in waves and build on each other. There are days where all you do is pour yourself out to your patients and you need someone to pour themselves into you, to refresh you, to make you laugh.

One night around 7 p.m. in the middle of flu season, I was sitting next to one of my partners finishing up some paperwork. We were exhausted. We had just counted up the number of patients each had seen that day and it was in the upper 60s. He and his wife are both Christians, have a good marriage, and have young children.

He called to tell her he would be home in about thirty minutes. She started yelling at him, "It's about time! I am so tired of the kids and I am waiting for you!" It went on for about two minutes. I could just see the life draining out of him. He hung up and looked over at me and said, "I guess you heard that."

So many thoughts went through my head. On the one hand, as the wife of a physician, I could totally identify with her. I vowed to never forget the look on his face and to try to remember it every time I was tempted to berate my husband when I was frustrated (I have failed too many times since). As a physician, I could identify with my partner as well, and I knew that he was in need of some refreshment from his spouse.

Both of these women, in totally different seasons of marriage, give real-life examples that we can easily relate to. They are absolutely right that exhaustion, both mental and physical, is a giant roadblock—a real enemy.

The time pressures that lead to exhaustion are real for both husband and wife. He has all the demands of a medical career. Many medical spouses also have busy careers that require a lot of time and energy. Most of us are consumed with raising children—a twenty-four hour, seven-day-a-week job. Many of us are doing both. Add to that the fact that we are the ones responsible for grocery shopping, cooking, cleaning, laundry, etc. Whew! So much to do in so little time sure does wear us out.

Few of us have husbands that work 9 a.m. to 5 p.m., allowing them to be home in the evening to help with household chores or with the children. If it were possible to work as a team to get those things done, then there would be more time to spend together. Unfortunately, unscheduled time is a luxury and rare commodity in a medical marriage. Exhaustion has a whole new meaning in our homes.

The fatigue is almost overwhelming at times for our husbands. I would not have thought it possible, if I did not witness it for myself. I recall an evening when I had prepared a special dinner and was eagerly awaiting spending some time with Ed over that meal. My anticipation turned to disappointment as I watched him begin to nod his head, followed by him laying his head down and actually falling asleep with his head on his dinner plate.

Another time, I was pleasantly surprised when he offered to watch our baby daughter while I cleaned up the kitchen after dinner. A short time later, Kristi came crawling into the kitchen. When I went to see where Ed was, I found him sound asleep on the family room floor, no pillow needed! I learned then not to depend on him to do anything—including talking—when he was exhausted.

Finding What Works

Some couples find ways to do things together that need to be done anyway. Running errands together for time to talk in the car, exercising together, and cooking together are examples of ways to maximize time. Ed and I both really enjoy our early morning walks several days a week that give us time to talk, exercise, and even pray together.

Having such limited time also makes it difficult to know how to bring up things on the "to do" list, which can be perceived as "nagging" and cause tension in the relationship. So, what do we do with the things we really need help with?

The right timing and the right words are so important in this situation. I found that saying something like, "I need help with a job that requires your strong muscles. I will patiently wait until you have time, but wanted you to be aware of this need," was helpful to both of us. It was not manipulative, but true. Ed appreciated being needed in a "manly" way, and I rarely had to wait long (though it sometimes felt like a long time to me).

One time, after one particular "brainstorming" session, we discovered that my making a list of things to be done and placing it on the refrigerator gave us both a sense of peace. I liked knowing the list was there when he was ready, and he liked that I didn't need to "remind" him. Ed was able to prioritize the list his way and then accomplish the tasks in his time frame. He really did get to everything on the "to do" list.

Scripture tells us, "Let us not become weary in doing good, for at the proper time we will reap a harvest if we do not give up" (Galatians 6:9). Remember that a wise woman looks for opportunities to bless her home by building her relationship with the husband God has given her. This brings her joy . . . and likely makes for a joyful husband, too!

There are many joys in being married to a doctor. You can likely think of several advantages right now . . . in fact, they will continue to delight and surprise you throughout your life. However, few of us are in need of help with handling the "good" parts. It is when we grow weary that advice and encouragement from others who understand our life become important—especially when that advice is based on the righteous, clear-focused instructions of God. These truths bring joy to our hearts.

What joy we have in Jesus who came to save us and will come again one day soon. What joy we bask in when our focus is on Him and His ways for our life. "Satisfy us in the morning with your unfailing love, that we may sing for joy and be glad all our days"

(Psalm 90:14). Make sure your heart is His. It connects you in such an incredible way to the Creator of the universe, to the Lover of your soul. Make sure you are listening to His truth. Trust Him. Obey Him. His promised joy, often unspeakable, will follow, overflowing into your home and through your life to the souls around you.

Rx: Restore balance to your life by making time first for what is truly most important to you.

Chapter 5

R

A Light Unto Your Path

Name :

Age :

Address :

Date :

The commands of the LORD are radiant, giving light to the eyes.

—Psalm 19:8b

Label ☐

Refill 0 1 2 3 4 5 PRN

H as your electricity ever gone off unexpectedly in the middle of the night? Have you ever been in a room so dark you couldn't see your own hand in front of your face? Did you have your flashlight handy? Were the batteries fresh? Maybe you preferred romantic candlelight to illuminate your space. Regardless of which method you chose, we all know the value of light when we are surrounded by darkness.

Rarely will you meet someone who prefers stumbling around in the dark, stubbing toes, bruising knees, bumping up against unseen objects. We read in Psalm 19:8 that His commands give light to the eyes. *The Message* phrases it this way, "The directions of GOD are plain and easy on the eyes." What a clear vision this verse gives us as to the purpose of His truth as it illuminates our way. His Word in us makes us both "alive" with this radiance and also "a light" to others around us.

In what areas do you need extra light these days? One challenge that many of us face is in the area of our personal finances. Another wonderful and mysterious subject to shine His light on would be prayer. Both of these areas of our lives reveal our true heart towards God. Fortunately, both topics are "well lit" for us in the Bible.

Light for Our Finances

God's Word is indeed "a lamp to my feet and a light for my path" (Psalm 119:105). Countless stories in the Bible teach us His practical truths and direction for our life about many things—including giving.

One such story unfolds in the Old Testament book of Haggai. The people of God had been facing drought, famine, and economic problems. Sound familiar? They were waiting for more prosperous times to build God's house. But Haggai, a prophet of God, went to Zerubbabel, the governor of Judah, and Joshua, the high priest, and said:

> These people say, "The time has not yet come to rebuild the LORD's house." . . . "Is it a time for you yourselves to be living in your paneled houses, while this house remains a ruin?
>
> . . . Give careful thought to your ways. You have planted much, but harvested little. You eat, but never have enough. You drink, but never have your fill. You put on clothes, but are not warm. You earn wages, only to put them in a purse with holes in it.
>
> . . . Give careful thought to your ways. Go up into the mountains and bring down timber and build my house, so that I may take pleasure in it and be honored," says the LORD. "You expected much, but see, it turned out to be little. What you brought home, I blew away. Why?" declares the LORD Almighty. "Because of my house, which remains a ruin, while each of you is busy with your own house. . . ." (Haggai 1:2-9).

The people in Haggai's time had set their own selfish interests above the priority of building the temple. They were probably thinking, "When we get this debt paid off, when we can afford our mortgage, when we have a little left over, then we will build the Lord's house." They had a lack of real spiritual commitment, likely leading to their economic problems. Today we are not building a literal building, but rather a living temple (see Ephesians 2:20-21). It is so easy for us to build our own homes and not invest our time, effort, talents, and finances in building God's kingdom. But His realm will last for eternity and it is vastly more important.

This is a struggle for me, too. I need to continually ask myself how I am doing with using the resources God has given me to build His kingdom—in my home, in my community, in my sphere of influence. My desire is to be a wise steward of what He has entrusted to me. I need to resist the temptation to reward myself with material things to feel better about the sacrifices of being a doctor's wife. I need to watch the tendency to rationalize that I "deserve" certain things.

That is not to say that we should lose sight of balance. God wants to give us good things and see us find pleasure in them—and especially in Him, the giver of the gifts. James 1:17 reminds us that every good and perfect gift is from Him.

A now elderly medical missionary's wife, well-acquainted with their often empty personal piggy bank, loved to say, "Oh, well. He owns the cattle on a thousand hills. I guess He can just sell one for us." And that seems to be what God did in all the stories she tells of His faithfulness.

A good guide for praying, no matter where you are financially, comes from Proverbs 30:8-9, "Give me neither poverty nor riches, but give me only my daily bread. Otherwise, I may have too much and disown you and say, 'Who is the LORD?' Or I may become poor and steal, and so dishonor the name of my God."

Trusting Him and not worrying when the money is tight is the best plan. Do we or don't we believe that familiar verse in Psalm 23:1, "The LORD is my shepherd. I shall not want?" Or, as it reads in *The Message*, "God, my shepherd! I don't need a thing." What a promise to confidently, courageously, and prayerfully claim as you declare your dependence on him.

Developing Good Habits

God deeply cares about where our heart is concerning everything—including our money and our time. God wants us to put Him and His priorities first. This requires much thought and prayer. When we are poor and greatly in debt during the medical school and residency years, the choices seem simple, as there is little money or time to spend on anything. This is an opportune moment to begin to form some habits that will make a huge difference later.

Ed and I were both students for the first two years of our marriage. He was in medical school, and I was finishing the last two years of my college nursing program. We learned to write down every expense, no matter how small. This helped us to see where our money was spent. We made decisions that we laugh about now like asking each other, "Are your shoe laces really bad enough to spend the money to buy new ones?" We learned much about being frugal then that we still apply in our lives today.

Not all medical students and residents are counting pennies, so search out and rub shoulders with other students who are practicing being frugal. One resident's wife put it this way, "Surround yourself with 'birds of a feather.'"

Exchanging ideas with those in the same situation in life really helped us in those early days. Asking questions like, "Where do you get your grocery bargains?" "What is your favorite thrift store?" and "Where can I get my hair cut reasonably?" are helpful. Today, there are also many websites that can aid your frugality.

Many couples choose to live on one income as much as possible so that they do not become dependent on two incomes when medical school and residency are behind them. There are many other creative ways to stretch your money. Ed and I chose to live with another couple, that also were both students, for our first year of marriage to share the expenses of the townhouse we were renting. Everyone said we would hate each other after that year together, but I am happy to say it worked out well and they are still good friends.

What is unique to us as medical spouses is that we often go from living at poverty level to earning a very comfortable income in less then ten years. In those early days, it can feel like survival-mode at times. Then comes the relief of a reasonable income. We may suddenly feel overwhelmed with how best to spend this income. That is when it is especially important to think, pray, and seek God's wisdom on this matter of where our "treasures lie" (see Matthew 6:19-21).

Be deliberate as you continue to make wise decisions that honor God as He blesses you with more of His resources for His use. The move from little to much can easily tempt us to be like the rich fool of Matthew 12 who greedily and fearfully stores it all up for his own security and his own purposes. The concluding wisdom of that parable could be summarized and embroidered on all our purses in this simple phrase: Be rich with what you have toward God.

What God Expects

God speaks to each of us differently as stewards of His resources. Ed and I often talked with our children, as we drove through our neighborhoods of larger homes, about the fact that the majority of the world did not live in affluence. We worked to serve the poor as a family. We gave financial support to mission organizations and ministries and urged our children to have missionary experiences in third-world countries and in our inner cities. We traveled as a family to serve together through medical missions in two different third-world countries. We tried to avoid the impulse to "keep up with the Joneses." At the same time, our desire was to avoid being critical of those with deeper pockets or those who spent their time and money differently.

In reading about the infamous Proverbs 31 woman, we get a good picture of one way to handle our money when there is plenty. Verse 20 says, "She opens her hands to the poor and extends her hands to the needy." In your generosity, not only are you giving directly to Jesus (see Matthew 25:31-46), but you are also demonstrating the fragrance of Christ to a hurting world.

Some of us are led to live in the inner city to influence our neighbors there. Others are called to local or overseas mission work. Many are called to use their income to support ministries, churches, and missions. The list goes on and on. The important question is, "What purpose does God have for the talents and money He has blessed me with?" I need to know His instructions concerning the use of my time, talents, and tithes.

PRESCRIPTION FOR THE DOCTOR'S WIFE

A dilemma exists when we have access to so much but don't take the time to develop a biblical perspective on our finances. It is hard, but so important, to set aside time to budget and handle our resources wisely instead of impulsively making purchases or unwise decisions. Many excellent books are available that can help you to manage your money. It is most helpful to consult those that give you a biblical perspective as soon as possible, if you haven't already.

In The Hole in Our Gospel, Richard Stearns, president of World Vision, asks, "What does God expect of us?" I was convicted, inspired, and motivated by his answers from Scripture. Stearns encourages us to embrace Jesus' heart for the poor and the vulnerable. Jesus wants us to see the needs and have compassion for the "least of these." He desires that we share His resources with a heart like His.

Brilliant light is shed on wealth in 1 Timothy 6:17-19: "Command those who are rich in this present world not to be arrogant nor to put their hope in wealth, which is so uncertain, but to put their hope in God, who richly provides us with everything for our enjoyment. Command them to do good, to be rich in good deeds, and to be generous and willing to share. In this way they will lay up treasure for themselves as a firm foundation for the coming age, so that they may take hold of the life that is truly life."

When I get off course in areas like spending, I am so grateful that God forgives me. He gives us a new start when we come to Him to repent of our ways. We need to ask ourselves the difficult questions: Have you found yourself believing that your security is your responsibility (or your husband's)? Have you found yourself worried about God's provision when the checkbook and the bills don't match up exactly as you had planned? Have worry, greed, or fear colored your financial outlook, and thus your heart, in a sinful way? Do you really need to purchase that new electronic gadget or that new piece of furniture? Is God your treasure or is it something else? These questions can cause us to search our hearts and make things right with God.

Fortunately, the children of God listened to Haggai when he them asked the tough questions. They repented. They heard God's message and quickly obeyed. The people got to work on God's house and they were blessed. Wow! Are we willing to listen to God and do the same?

Outside the Box

God led Ed and me to make a decision that did not make much financial sense by the world's standards. We had a choice to be obedient or not. We decided to follow Him and the blessings were—and continue to be—abundant.

After Ed had practiced emergency medicine for twenty years, we both sensed God calling us to minister in a different way. We had long desired to make an impact for God's kingdom together. We loved the community where we lived and felt God was using us there to minister to others. We had been involved in various ministries through our church and in our community. One that was particularly fulfilling to us was working with medical couples. After having watched so many medical marriages fail and so many physicians burn out due to their profession, we felt a real burden to make an eternal difference in these lives. We had struggled at times, too, and wanted to come alongside of others with the comfort and guidance that God had given us.

As we spent the next two years praying and seeking God's leading, He brought us to a crossroads. We chose the path that we believed God was illuminating. It meant giving up a practice with a well-paying job where Ed was a partner. It also meant moving to a new area, as we felt led to work with medical students and residents, and there was no medical school associated with the university near our home.

We sensed God was leading Ed to practice emergency medicine for half of his vocational time and use the remainder to minister to those who practiced medicine. I felt called to minister with him to those in healthcare. We knew the pay would be significantly less. But God opened doors as only He can. Christian Medical and Dental Associations welcomed us with open arms to serve together as one staff person (each being half time) as co-directors of the Campus and Community Ministry for the Richmond, Virginia, area. God provided a lovely home on a lake that allows us to use our home for fellowship, events, and retreats. Ed found a wonderful part-time position that allows him to minister to the patients he cares for. The best part is he also gets to interact with medical students, graduates, and residents in a teaching setting, as well as interact with practicing doctors that are his colleagues.

The incredible blessings we have experienced since making this significant change are too numerous to count. The opportunity to work with medical, dental, pharmacy, physical therapy, occupational therapy, and nursing students has been inspiring, challenging, and extremely rewarding. We are inadequate, but God's grace and the faithful prayers of the Christian medical community here have made awesome things happen. God is the one making the difference here. Lives are being changed and His Kingdom is being built.

No matter what God's plan for your life and ministry may be, the answer is always to seek His direction for your resources. Even the challenges and struggles will become tools to help you grow in your faith. The joys and blessings will be "abundantly more than you could ask or imagine" (see Ephesians 3:20)!

The Privilege of Prayer

It takes maturing of our faith to come to the realization that the resources we have in life are really entrusted to us by God for His use. A powerful tool He has given us is prayer. Paul reminded us to "pray continually" (1 Thessalonians 5:17). This means talking to God throughout each day—praising Him, thanking Him, interceding on behalf of others, and bringing our own joys and concerns to Him.

In the Old Testament, we learn that Daniel considered this priority so important that he willingly risked his life to pray three times a day. Daniel had such exceptional leadership qualities that King Darius planned to set him over the whole kingdom. The king's crooked administrators didn't want this, but they couldn't find any corruption in Daniel to disqualify him. So they passed a law that everyone had to worship the king, knowing Daniel would refuse, as he worshipped God alone.

"Now when Daniel learned that the decree had been published, he went home to his upstairs room where the windows opened toward Jerusalem. Three times a day he got down on his knees and prayed, giving thanks to his God, just as he had done before" (Daniel 6:10). Incredible! No wonder he was found "trustworthy" and was spiritually prepared for every situation. Because of Daniel's faithfulness, our awesome God protected and delivered him from the lion's den (Daniel's punishment for praying to God and not bowing to King Darius).

There is nothing quite as important as starting our day with God. It helps us to begin our day with the right priorities and right focus. Jesus called Himself the "bread of life" (John 6:35). Each day I make it a priority to eat three meals—my "daily bread." Yet, do I make it a priority to have the true bread that I need—time with Jesus—at least three times a day too? Scripture tells us, "Very early in the morning, while it was still dark, Jesus got up, left the house, and went off to a solitary place where he prayed" (Mark 1:35). Just think . . . if Jesus needed this time of prayer, then how much more do we!

Nothing else has the power, the protection, the provision, and the potential to change our lives that prayer does. God changes us through prayer. He also changes our hearts toward circumstances and other people as we pray for them—especially our husbands.

Our husbands are in great need of our prayers. You may find the following suggestions helpful as you lift your man up before the Lord. If you add ten prayers of your own, there will be enough for you to focus on one request each day of the month. Incorporate these things along with what you have already been praying for him. It is a powerful privilege to do so!

His Relationship with God

1. That he would love God with all his heart, soul, mind, and strength (Mark 12:30-31).
2. That the Lord would be his strength and shield (Psalm 28:7).
3. That the Lord would instruct and teach him in the way he should go (Psalm 32:8).
4. That he would mediate on God's Word (Psalm 1:1-3).
5. That God would keep his way pure by his knowing and keeping God's Word (Psalm 119:9-11).
6. That his eyes would be fixed on Jesus—the author and perfecter of his faith (Hebrews 12:2).

7. For strength and protection from the Evil One (2 Thessalonians 3:3).

His Relationship with You, His Wife

1. That he would love his wife as Christ loved the church (Ephesians 5:25).
2. That he would be considerate of his wife so that nothing would hinder his prayers (1 Peter 3:7).

His Relationship with His Family

1. That he would be strong and courageous, obeying God, that he might be a successful leader of his family (Joshua 1:7).
2. That he would manage his family well (1 Timothy 3:4).
3. That he would impress God's commands on his children (Deuteronomy 6:6-7).
4. That he would be quick to listen, slow to speak and slow to become angry (James 1:19).
5. In the area of finances, that he would desire to "store up treasures in heaven" (Matthew 6:19-21).
6. That he would balance priorities in his life from a biblical perspective (Psalm 39:5-6).

His Relationships with Other Men

1. For strong relationships with other men (Hebrews 10:24).

2. That his time with other men would be like "iron sharpening iron" (Proverbs 27:17).

His Work

1. That he would distinguish himself through his character qualities (Daniel 6:3).

2. That God would bless the work of his hands (Proverbs 90:17).

3. That he "would go out to preach the kingdom of God and to heal the sick" (Luke 9:2).

Don't believe Satan's lies that prayer is a "duty." Don't give in to the deception that tempts us to say, "I don't feel like praying." Remember, the times we really don't feel like praying are the times we need to pray the most. Join me in making the commitment to pray daily for our dear husbands who desperately need our prayers! Let's pray for wisdom and in faith (see James 1:5-8), that we might receive what we ask for as we obey (see 1 John 3:22) and remain in Him (see John 15:7).

Focused on Him

The truth is that we have the awesome privilege of approaching our Holy God who sits on His throne of grace . . . ready and eager for us to come to Him. The God of the universe wants an intimate, personal relationship with each one of us. He cares deeply about what is on our minds and in our hearts. Incredible!

Oswald Chambers said, "When a man is born from above, the life of the Son of God is born in him, and he can either starve that life or nourish it. Prayer is the way the life of God is nourished. Our ordinary views of prayer are not found in the New Testament. We look upon prayer as a means of getting things for ourselves; the Bible's idea of prayer is that we may get to know God Himself."

Prayer is not demanding what we want from God. Instead it is focused on Him and seeking His will. 1 John 5:14-15 says, "This is the confidence we have in approaching God: that if we ask anything according to his will, he hears us. And if we know that he hears us—whatever we ask—we know that we have what we have asked of him." By prayer, we seek God's will and yield to it.

Do you struggle at times with knowing how to pray for a particular situation or person? I sure do! I find much comfort in Romans 8:26 that assures me, "In the same way, the Spirit helps us in our weakness. We do not know what we ought to pray for, but the Spirit himself intercedes for us with groans that words cannot express."

E. M. Bounds has written extensively about prayer. He explains this concept about the Spirit interceding well. He said, "The Holy Spirit helps us in our weaknesses, gives wisdom to our ignorance, turns ignorance into wisdom, and changes our weakness into strength. The Spirit Himself does this. He helps and takes hold with us as we tug and toil . . . He pleads for us and in us. He quickens, illumines, and inspires our prayers. He proclaims and elevates the matter of our prayers, and inspires the words and feelings of our prayers. He works mightily in us so that we can pray mightily. He enables us to pray always and ever according to the will of God."

At any time and place we can come before God with boldness because of Jesus' shed blood on our behalf. Aren't you thankful that God has given us the gift of open communication with Him? He has also given us the gift of His Spirit to help us when we don't know how to pray. How incredibly blessed we are! Doesn't this make you want to fall to your knees and start praying now?

The Best Answer

Recently, my granddaughter, Megan, had one of those nasty gastrointestinal viruses. Shortly after vomiting, she began begging her mom for waffles with whipped cream on them. She cried and pleaded as only a three-year-old can. Kristi refused her request because she knew it was not best for Megan. How thankful I am that God says no to my harmful requests. I am so grateful that God knows what is best for me and answers my prayers according to His perfect will. It might be "yes" or "no" or "wait," but it is always right and just.

God has miraculously answered many of my prayers. I am so grateful for these times, as they have brought Him glory! Several years ago I had a bowel obstruction that occurred very suddenly. Hours of pain and vomiting sent me to the ER. I was admitted to the hospital and seen by the surgeon. Many people were praying for me. I certainly was praying too!

During a sleepless night, I prayed and asked God to untwist the bowel—which would prevent me from needing surgery. I confessed He was still God if He chose not to answer "yes" and that I trusted that He knew what was best for me. I wanted to glorify Him either way. The next morning, a physician who is a member of our local CMDA council prayed for me in the hallway outside the radiology department. I sensed a change in my body.

When I went back to my room, I felt well enough to work on my Bible study lesson on James. As I read chapter 5, I sensed God telling me that the prayer that had been offered in faith would make me well and that the prayer of a righteous man was indeed powerful and effective. I believed that my prayers and the prayers of others were answered.

I shared this with several visitors, who kindly suggested that I not get my hopes up as the x-ray clearly showed I did indeed need surgery. I shared this with my doctor who listened to my story with a perplexed expression. I shared this with my night nurse and told her that by morning the surgery would be canceled due to evidence that the bowel was functioning. This nurse was a believer and rejoiced with me when it became evident that I would no longer need the surgery. Praise God for His miraculous healing hand!

How I enjoyed watching my doctor's face as he declared that I no longer needed surgery. He had seen the hand of God at work and we had an amazing conversation. Neither of us were the same after that remarkable experience.

How about you? What are your stories of answered prayer? Have there been times when in the end you were thankful that God, in His infinite wisdom, did not simply say "yes" to your prayers? Were there times when He moved mightily and miraculously on your behalf? Let's remember these and praise God for the power and privilege we have in prayer! Let's bend our knees and bring our hearts before Him.

Seek Him First

Where do you turn *first* for help? Maybe the washing machine is broken. Maybe your head is aching. Maybe your baby won't stop crying. Maybe you have a huge challenge at work. Maybe your extended family is causing you to fret over a difficult situation. Maybe you just feel a little discouraged. Life needs fixing. Life needs answers. Sometimes those answers are needed *right now.*

In my own personal dramas, unsolvable problems, mental complexities, physically painful challenges, emotional upheavals, and financial fears, I can't tell you how many times I have run *first* to the less-skilled, less-equipped, or non-expert resource. Wouldn't it make more sense if first I went to the *Source?* The One in whom I have confidence, the One with the unimpeachable track record?

I really believe that God means it when He says, "But seek first his kingdom and his righteousness, and all these things will be given to you as well" (Matthew 6:33). I believe that the key is knowing that God is the expert in all things, all situations, and all challenges. I'm not saying that others don't play an important role in our lives. Our friends and family can impart true wisdom, but anytime they become the final answer—before I've consulted the Expert—I am off course.

Where should I turn first? "I lift up my eyes to the mountains— where does my help come from? My help comes from the LORD, the Maker of heaven and earth" (Psalm 121:1-2). In the end, only God knows the who, what, when, where, how, and why of all that stretches me in life. He is my confidence. He is the Great I Am! He is the mysterious, loving, in control, righteous, holy know-it-all!

Listen. Can you hear God calling your name? He is waiting with unlimited time to talk over your problems—the immediate ones and the ones you fear may be just around the corner. Hear Him speak to you as you come into His presence: "My child, have no fear of sudden disaster or of the ruin that overtakes the wicked, I will be your confidence and will keep your foot from being snared. But blessed are you, my child; don't be afraid. What can man do to you? This is the confidence you have in approaching Me: that you ask anything according to My will, I hear!" (see Proverbs 3:25-26; Jeremiah 17:7; Hebrews 13:6; 1 John 5:14).

One of my favorite songs says, "God will make a way, when there seems to be no way. He works in ways we cannot see. He will make a way for me. He will be my guide. Hold me closely to His side. With love and strength for each new day, He will make a way. . . . He will make a way."

Dear friend, rest in these comforting words and in His truths. Go first to Him. Go often to Him. "Do not be anxious about anything, but in everything, by prayer and petition, with thanksgiving, present your requests to God. And the peace of God, which transcends all understanding, will guard your hearts and minds in Christ Jesus" (Philippians 4:6-7).

Rx: Spend time every day in prayer and ask God to illuminate His plans for your life

Rx

Chapter 6

Learning to Trust

Name :

Age :

Address :

Date :

The fear of the LORD is pure, enduring forever.

—Psalm 19:9a

Label ☐

Refill 0 1 2 3 4 5 PRN

Refill 0 1 2 3 4 5 PRN

What makes your hands get clammy and your heart race? Snakes, spiders, or maybe a mouse? Perhaps your stomach clenches up at the thought of losing your job. Maybe you worry constantly about something happening to a loved one. Or possibly a great suspense movie keeps you on the edge of your seat as you apprehensively wait to see what lurks around the darkened corner.

Fear! We all know the feeling, for we have all experienced it at one time or another. But more than just an emotion of terror, worry, or suspense, *Webster's* also defines *fear* as a "profound reverence and awe—especially toward God." We are called to revere God alone as we go about our daily lives. As we think about all that He has powerfully and magnificently done and continues to do, we need not fear other people, circumstances, or the unknown. He wants us to put our whole trust in Him.

Glowing sunsets, sweeping mountain vistas, and colorful autumn brilliance are scenes that fill me with awe. What about the sights, sounds, and sweet smells of a newborn baby? Are you filled with wonder by the Creator's touch in all of these miraculous gifts? I certainly am! This kind of fear—directed toward our Maker, our Provider, our perfect Bridegroom—when consistently focused on

Him, can keep my soul free from impurity, harboring nothing inappropriate or extraneous. It is pure. It endures forever because *He* does. It does not change because *He* won't. Our response can't help but be one of amazement and awe of our glorious God!

Look around you. What do you see in your world that inspires the reverential fear of God in your heart today? Do you see Him for who He is or are you misdirecting that fear, allowing other things to control your world? Is He big enough to trust every day and with every thing? Indeed He is, but we must choose whether to trust Him or not.

We Are Never Alone

Many times, my husband is not available when I need him. Does this happen to you, too? Why does is seem that the really big or difficult problems always seem to come up when our husbands are not at home to help us? Perhaps, it is to compel me to run to God instead of my first inclination, which is to run to my man.

Our smoke alarm going off in the middle of the night was not welcome when, of course, my resident husband was on call at the hospital. The piercing sound was definitely effective. I awoke immediately. Unfortunately, I had no clue how to stop the shrill noise. I checked on our sleeping baby, looked all around the house, and finally figured out how to dismantle the alarm. Nothing was on fire, but I was unable to go back to sleep due to worrying that I might have overlooked some smoke.

You may have experienced similar feelings to those I had that night. We may be especially vulnerable to fear because as medical spouses, we spend many hours alone, especially at night. We cannot easily call our husbands for reassurance or expect them to simply leave the hospital to help with our crisis. We may feel dreadfully alone.

I spent many hours in a useless state of worry before I began to believe the verses I was saying to myself over and over. A favorite for nights like the smoke alarm episode was, "I will lie down and sleep in peace, for you alone, O LORD, make me dwell in safety" (Psalm 4:8). It brought me great comfort to remember "he . . . will neither slumber nor sleep" (Psalm 121:3-4). God would tenderly watch over my baby and me—doing a much better job than I ever could. On nights like this, peaceful sleep came when my focus was on Him.

When I am tempted to let myself become paralyzed by fear I must refocus on Him as my mighty sovereign Creator. His character is fully trustworthy. For isn't He the most awesome of all beings? When I reflect on Him as the truest lover of my soul and caretaker of my well-being, my confidence in Him grows.

Trusting is easy when things are manageable, but what about when situations are totally beyond our ability to handle? When circumstances around me look dismal, I can say, as Isaiah did, "I will wait for the Lord . . . I will put my trust in Him" (Isaiah 8:17). God continues to teach me much about His trustworthiness as I read the Bible and walk this life with Him. Trust is a choice. Unfortunately, I am a rather slow learner in this area. But God has shown me in miraculous ways what He can do when I trust Him.

Out of Control

The hardest times for me to trust God were those that involved the needs of my children. Life with little ones was full and fun, and I was happiest when I was in control and had everything organized.

Structure and routine are certainly very helpful with small children, but things could get out of balance quickly whenever I thought I was in charge and forgot that God alone was in perfect control. I learned a valuable lesson about the importance of trusting Him when our oldest daughter, Kristi, was just four years old.

We were stationed in Guam with the Navy and had just welcomed our third child, Jon, when Kristi developed a congenital cholesteatoma—a benign tumor—in her right ear. She needed an emergency flight to California to receive treatment, because Guam did not have the necessary surgical intervention. Kristi was already losing her hearing in that ear, so time was critical.

Only one person could accompany Kristi on the flight. Jon was two months old at the time, and I was nursing him. Since Jon would have counted as a second person, I could not go. Fortunately, Ed was given permission to take time off to travel with her. I was very grateful for this and knew that his medical expertise would be very valuable. But my daughter was about to have major surgery five thousand miles away, and I was not going to be there for her! I was distraught, to say the least.

God taught me more than you can imagine during that time, and my heart was forever changed. God brought Kristi safely through the surgery and recovery, and Ed was blessed to have some much-needed time to bond with his daughter. I gained a greater appreciation for my dear husband and his medical knowledge— truly it is a gift from the Lord to have a doctor in the family when there is a medical crisis!

Those were blessings enough, but the full scope of God's faithfulness was miraculously revealed over the following months as I sought to trust Him rather than focus on the "circumstances." The damage caused by the tumor had been extensive and Kristi lost hearing in her right ear. (I am so grateful that God gives us two ears!) She no longer had an eardrum, and her doctors told us she would have difficulty swimming or showering, because any water getting in that ear would make her very dizzy. We prayed that God would somehow give us an answer to this problem.

It wasn't long before Ed's assignment in Guam came to an end, and we visited the ENT doctor in Guam before heading back to the States. He said that Kristi was healing very well and commented that she had an amazingly well-attached skin graft inside her ear. Ed was baffled. The damage had been too extensive for any surgical repair, and he looked at the doctor in confusion and said, "No graft was done."

The doctor said, "Look for yourself," which Ed did. He had done this many times before, but this time he was astonished to see a beautifully formed piece of skin that only God could have placed there. This miracle meant she would be able to swim, bathe, and participate in every other normal activity. Gratitude and praise overflowed from our hearts. Only God could have met Kristi's needs so fully. How thankful I was that I was not the one "in control" during that situation!

Can you recount a similar story of God's provision and blessing in your life? Or are some situations still in the "trusting and waiting" stage? It can be particularly challenging to trust God when it seems circumstances will never change. Kristi's miracle came about relatively quickly, but at other times, I have had to trust and wait much, much longer.

One story of God's faithfulness that was years in the making concerned my relationship with my parents. Not long after I became a believer, I shared my new faith with my parents. They were extremely upset and were sure I had joined a cult. It took eighteen long years of saying few words and attempting, through my actions, to live my faith before them. What a joyous day it was when each of them understood God's good news and believed in Jesus. Their personal faith was evident to all—especially in the peace they had in their final days on earth, despite the ravages of cancer. It seemed like a long wait by my human standards, but God was faithful in His perfect way and in His perfect time.

Hope in Brokenness

Even though the endings of some of our stories of God's faithfulness have yet to be written, it is helpful to remember we are not alone. How many heroes of the Bible had "hanging on" assigned to them as they longed for all things to be made right and clear? Most!

We need to trust Him as we follow Him and wait for Him to show us the answers. Psalm 27:14 tells us to "Wait for the LORD; be strong and take heart and wait for the LORD." God knows it is hard for us to rest in His timing, so He reminds us to be strong and take heart. Our confidence is in the Lord who delivers us.

This truth was particularly helpful to someone very close to me who had trust vows broken in her marriage. Unfortunately, this happens all too often in medical marriages. The husband is often away from home. Maybe a nurse he works with becomes a temptation. A wife discovers her husband is addicted to pornography—an all too common scenario. Or the wife is lonely and looks for attention from someone else, because her husband can't meet her needs. It often begins innocently enough—a listening ear, a shoulder to lean on. But one step in the wrong direction followed by another can quickly lead to unfaithfulness. Oh, may we guard our hearts and run for help to Him, our Strong Tower!

Yes, the truth is human trust can be broken—and often is. The pain is intense. Many have described the hurt as being like a death. In many ways, it is like a hemorrhage slowly seeping away the body's life-source. Trust is critical to a healthy marriage. For when it is broken, the devastation causes severe damage to the foundation that the marriage is built upon.

Fortunately, through God's grace and with time, it is possible for the health of a marriage to be rebuilt even better and stronger than before. Clinging to the truth of God's Word enables us to go on. Meeting with mentors who can pray for us and hold us accountable is crucial. Memorizing appropriate verses to meditate on empowers us to "hang in there." It takes much hard work and both partners must keep their focus on God, as He alone can heal a marriage. He is trustworthy when we are not. He is dependable when we are not.

The Bible says, "He has sent me to bind up the brokenhearted, to proclaim freedom for the captives and release from darkness for the prisoners, to proclaim the year of the LORD's favor and the day of vengeance of our God, to comfort all who mourn, and provide for those who grieve in Zion—to bestow on them a crown of beauty instead of ashes, the oil of joy instead of mourning, and a garment of praise instead of a spirit of despair" (Isaiah 61:1-3). Praise the Lord! He can take even a pile of ashes and make something beautiful!

We are reminded, as well, in Colossians 3:13 to "Bear with each other and forgive whatever grievances you may have against one another. Forgive as the Lord forgave you." Trusting in God who sees all, the eternal Alpha and Omega, and applying His Word to our life changes our attitude from bitterness and hopelessness to one of peace. We can cling to Him as the Author and Finisher of our faith, according to Hebrews 12:2, knowing He truly can see it all.

There is a temptation to turn away from God when difficulties come. After all, how could a loving God allow something like this to happen? Rest assured that He is absolutely in control. The Enemy of our souls knows this world is broken, and he takes full advantage of that reality. He wants nothing more than for us to stay mired in anger, bitterness, hopelessness, and doubt. But healing and hope come as we run to God, over and over again, in total dependence.

Sin entered this world because God allowed us free will. Mercifully, He had a plan of redemption in place to bring us back to a right relationship with Him. Here was the very first situation of broken trust—and rather than destroy this rebelling man and woman, God chose to set a series of events in motion that would bring about full restoration. He chose to proclaim the grace that lay ahead through a promised seed, Jesus. Generously, He also gave us His Word to guide us through every hardship and every effect of sin that we face.

Jesus' willingness to endure the cross for me and for you has offered us our greatest hope. Someday we will be with Him for all of eternity. Job, at one of the lowest points in his life, said, "I know that my Redeemer lives, and that in the end he will stand upon the earth. And after my skin has been destroyed, yet in my flesh I will see God" (Job 19:25-26). Job's words proclaim the hope we have no matter what is happening in our lives. He knew that this life is preparation for the next life. He knew that there is promise of a better place— our heavenly home!

This certainly changes our perspective. In Revelation 15:3-4 the song of the Lamb is sung. "Great and marvelous are your deeds, Lord God Almighty. Just and true are your ways, King of the ages. Who will not fear you, O Lord, and bring glory to your name? For you alone are holy." Picture that scene and rejoice in the ultimate hope we have! The magnificence of the reality of heaven is beyond my comprehension, but what I do understand gives me hope beyond words.

Remember Your History

If you are like me, your history with someone causes your confidence in that person to be built up or torn down. The trust I have for my husband has grown tremendously over the years as we have experienced the highs and lows of life together. We have disappointed each other at times, causing us to doubt the person we are trusting in. As the Bible says, "We all, like sheep, have gone astray" (Isaiah 53:6). But thankfully, there is One who will always be worthy of our trust who we can turn to; One whose way is always perfect.

Our confidence is not in something, but in Someone. We were redeemed with the precious blood of Jesus. Our Savior, Friend, and the One who sticks closer than a brother. "Through Him you believe in God, who raised him from the dead and glorified him, and so your faith and hope are in God" (1 Peter 1:21).

When we begin a life with God, we are given the wonderful benefit of rich history with Him. Only then can our trust in Him grow deeper. What does your "God history book" look like? Do you have His trustworthy acts stored in your heart and mind? Do you have parts of it written down? Do you spend time reviewing it? Journaling is well worth the time, even in the simplest of forms. In other words, do you deliberately meditate on your history with the One who created you, knows everything about you, and loves you more than anyone else ever could?

God, the Master Journal Keeper, did not sugarcoat the lives of those He chose to include. You may remember the story of the Samaritan woman who was drawing water when the Savior approached. Jesus tenderly, lovingly conversed with her in spite of all her cultural baggage and her broken life. In the end this woman, with incredulous neighbors and dusty disciples looking on, couldn't stop exclaiming, "He knows everything about me!"

One of the saddest themes running through the stories of God's people in the Old Testament is that they frequently forgot what He had done for them. Most of us know of the miraculous account of the parting of the Red Sea after God's children had been freed from slavery in Egypt. Imagine the trust built in these people as He miraculously triumphed over Pharaoh's army! Unfortunately, Exodus 15 goes on to describe how Israel's glorious praise of God quickly turned to grumbling when they forgot His mighty deeds.

This happens to us, too, when we forget how honorable and faithful He is. We struggle when we fail to remember our history with Him. We stumble and fall when our eyes are on our circumstances and not on His faithfulness to us.

Past, Present, Future—He Has Them All Covered

When I lean on my own strength or understanding, which I do all too often, I am in peril. I desire to live out the truth of Scripture and must remind myself that He alone is trustworthy. I need to focus on verses like Psalm 62:8: "Trust in him at all times, O people; pour out your hearts to him, for God is our refuge."

Our God is unshakably dependable. Run first for help to Him, remembering His faithfulness in the past. Life does not surprise Him or make Him wonder what will happen next. He has promised to care for every need. He will be steadfast in His loving care.

American pastor and modern-day prophet A.W. Tozer reflected on this very truth. "God perfectly knows Himself, and, being the source and author of all things, it follows that He knows all that can be known. And this He knows instantly and with a fullness of perfection that includes every possible item of knowledge concerning everything that exists or could have existed anywhere in the universe at any time in the past or that may exist in the centuries or ages yet unborn. God knows instantly and effortlessly all matter and all matters, all mind and every mind . . . all relations, all cause, all thoughts, all mysteries, all enigmas, all feeling, all desires, every unuttered secret, all thrones and dominions, all personalities, all things visible and invisible in heaven and in earth, motion, space, time, life, death, good, evil, heaven, and hell."

One of the verses I most often share with others is Romans 15:13, "May the God of hope fill you with all joy and peace as you trust in Him, so that you may overflow with hope by the power of the Holy Spirit." We need this verse because we live in a broken world where things seem beyond recovery at times. It reminds us to relinquish our own desires and concerns and give more power to the Holy Spirit who indwells us by yielding more fully to Him. Then we will overflow with confident assurance by His power.

We need God's hope to continue on when our life seems shaken or shattered, hope that brings us peace and joy is the fruit of trusting in Him. This hope and trust are often seen together in Scripture—because they are essential for our mental and spiritual health. Few things are sadder than a woman without God's optimism for her tomorrows.

In *Loving God With All Your Mind,* Elizabeth George puts it this way: "Have you ever met a woman with bright eyes and a ready smile whose positive outlook on life gives her contagious energy? Her secret may be knowing that God's great love for her means that everything that happens to her—in the present as well as the past and in the future—will be good in the hands of her heavenly Father. This kind of women is confident that God watches over every aspect of her life, and she greets every event with this knowledge."

Conversely, we know how being crippled with fear, filled with anxiety, and lacking a God-focused confidence affects not only us, but also those around us. Note the "strength and dignity" that clothes the Proverbs 31 woman (verse 25), allowing her to "laugh at the days to come." She is free of worry and anxiety.

Isaiah 41:10 instructs us, "So do not fear, for I am with you; do not be dismayed, for I am your God. I will strengthen you and help you; I will uphold you with my righteous right hand." What a beautiful reminder. When we picture Him holding us in His hand, fear subsides. Peace increases.

Of course, this is not always easy. Unfortunately, we often spend so much time dwelling on the past, feeling discontent in the present, or worrying about the future that we can miss seeing what God is doing in our lives right now. We may feel forgotten or overlooked and wonder if God really cares about us. One dear young woman experienced those very struggles during her husband's medical school and residency years.

Aaron and I met during his sophomore year of college. We started dating the following year and about a year later were talking about getting engaged. Aaron had wanted to be a medical missionary since he was in middle school. He dreamed about living in the jungle, making alternative medicines, and serving indigenous people.

Aaron is a planner. Though we felt our lives were heading in the same direction, he wanted me to talk to a doctor's wife to make sure I knew what I was getting into.

I met with a wonderful woman who was married to an ER doctor. She was very honest with me, warning me about the pressures of medical school and residency. She told me very honestly about her husband's relationship with her kids and the stresses that being a doctor put on the whole family.

With stars in my eyes, I "took in" what she was saying without really processing how this similar road might actually affect my life. I think we're all prone to think *my husband will be different* or *my experiences will be better.* I foolishly fell into this camp.

Aaron and I got married after he graduated and then took a year off between undergraduate and medical school while I finished my degree. He worked with Campus Crusade for Christ during that year, something that was a huge blessing but would become a point of contention down the road. After I graduated we moved to a new town, where I took a job as a structural engineer and Aaron started medical school. While he reveled in anatomy, I began to feel like I was drowning and forgotten.

During this time I realized that I had expectations that I had never verbalized or processed. While I always knew Aaron was going to medical school, I never anticipated what the ramifications of that decision would be. I never really wanted to work as an engineer, but we were facing a lot of medical school debt and of course we had living expenses. We decided that I would take on the burden of working and also running the home. I wanted Aaron to be free to concentrate on medical school. I knew he had a lot to learn and only a little time to learn it. I wanted him to be successful and I felt bad asking him to do anything but study.

The wisest choice, at the time, was to take the job that would provide best for our family. I was blessed with a wonderful boss and a generous salary. But I wasn't working out of my strengths and I felt increasingly burdened by the weight of responsibility I had taken on.

It only took a few months for me to become overwhelmed and resentful. I felt trapped in a job that I didn't enjoy. We couldn't move, I couldn't go back to school, and I was limited by the jobs that were available near Aaron's medical school. I started to resent how much he enjoyed what he was doing and how much I had to sacrifice to support his dream. It didn't help that his previous job with Campus Crusade was a job I longed to have but was not available where we lived.

On top of the job issue, I started to realize my long-term plans weren't really feasible. I dreamed Aaron would finish school and residency, we would move overseas, take on the adventure of medical missions together and then a few years later would think about starting a family. And we had been dreaming about having a big family. In fact, we both hoped the Lord would bless us with six children.

One day I started thinking about our future family and it suddenly occurred to me. *We'll be thirty when Aaron finishes residency!* Now thirty isn't old, but if after residency we take a few years to pay off our debt then move overseas and minister for a few years, how old would we be before we thought about kids? I mean, did we really want to start a big family when we were nearing forty? Something had to give. Either the number of children we wanted or the timing of starting a family.

In the end, we decided we valued having a big family and endeavored to start having children. But in this decision I had to mourn the plans I had for my life. I had to accept that my role in our overseas mission might look very different than I had dreamed. It seemed my primary role would be that of a mom, not a missionary. It's something I am now very excited about. But in a time where I longed to work in something I loved, it was a bittersweet indication of our present reality. It seemed once again, Aaron would be living my dream, and I would have to adjust to support him. To add insult to injury, Aaron's schedule picked up as he transitioned from classes to clinical rotations. One thing after another seemed to stack up, and I ended up feeling utterly forgotten. Forgotten by Aaron, by the world, and mostly by God. I knew these were lies, but the feelings remained powerful.

Now, a few years later, as I reflect on those feelings, I realize how quickly God can change not only your circumstances but also your heart. With six months left in medical school Aaron gave me the freedom to quit my job. I took time off to explore other jobs and to recuperate from an emotionally difficult time. Then a month before Aaron's residency began I was offered a new job in my old company that perfectly utilized my natural strengths. The entire situation was a huge blessing that I could not have planned in my wildest dreams. My boss paid to have me take some career aptitude tests to make sure that my strengths would line up with the new job he was offering me. He then paid to get me some additional training so that I could do this job well.

Quite literally, out of nowhere, I was offered a job that was not on my radar and was beyond what I could imagine. And the reason I was offered that job was because of the years that I had worked in a job that didn't fit my skills and because of the step of faith Aaron and I took to look into other options. I was not forgotten at all.

The Lord saw me, knew my strengths, and was working in my circumstances to give me greater insight into those strengths and weaknesses. I also believe the Lord graciously gave me a job I enjoyed so much to further show me how much He cared about me and my circumstances.

As far as our family plans . . . well that's something the Lord is still working out. But the change in my plans that caused us to start trying to have a family showed us a few invaluable things. First, we found out we have infertility issues. While this has been difficult, I cannot imagine what it would have been like to find this out ten years from now. Also, since it's taken us longer to start a family, I've had time to process my desire to be a mom. A life that I once mourned is now something I truly long for. We discovered all of these truths because the Lord brought us on a path that was different from my desires, but was perfect based on what we needed.

Hindsight is always 20/20. But as I look back on our time in medical school, and even the beginning of residency, I'm overwhelmed by the realization that God loves us, remembers us, and has our best in mind. If things had gone my way, then I never would have experienced the invaluable lessons, the wonderful gifts of friendship, and the intimacy with Aaron that God desired for me. We rarely ask for difficult circumstances, but we often ask for the character development that comes as a result of them.

We're not sure what the future holds, but we do know that this time, though difficult, was perfect. Our future circumstances will hold their own challenges, but we are a bit better prepared for them because we've been made a little bit more like the only One who is perfect. And for that, we're grateful.

This young woman clearly felt forgotten, even despairing at times, yet now she has a more vibrant history with her always-dependable God. She has personally experienced His lavish love and compassionate care that fills her with great expectations for the future.

May we grow more and more as we consistently rely on God, letting Him build confident trust in our hearts that will overflow to the relationships inside and outside of our homes. His care for us is so amazing and His love for us is so unfathomable! I praise God who is perfectly adequate and fully worthy of my complete trust.

The Road to Hope

Is there a situation in your life that seems hopeless? The pain of a broken relationship? A child who is living in rebellion? Feeling utterly stuck in a role or a job? A husband with wrong priorities? Boldly bring them all to Him and wait patiently for His answers, (see Romans 15:4).

Some years ago, I was personally burdened concerning a work situation that seemed to be consuming my husband. The circumstances seemed to blind him to the needs of his family and other priorities around him. At first, I made excuses for him, thinking it would be temporary. Then I did what I should have done from the beginning—I began to pray for him. I admit the hard part was to then wait patiently for God to do what only He can do.

God had an amazing lesson for my husband that I am so thankful I didn't ruin by trying to intervene, though I sure was tempted to. When all of Ed's time and effort invested in starting a new clinic fell through due to an administrative decision, he was crushed. However, God used it in a mighty way to help him get his priorities back to a godly balance. He had a real-life lesson in the importance of investing time and energy in what really mattered for eternity. This experience still impacts him today, as is evident by the quote he places at the end of his e-mails: "Our greatest fear as individuals. . . should not be of failure but of succeeding at things in life that don't really matter" (Tim Kizziar).

My lesson was in learning the value of waiting on God's timing. I longed for Ed to see that his priorities were out of balance. Naturally, I felt I would be the best one to correct this imbalance, which, of course, meant moving me up to second priority on his list! (I did want God to be first priority for my husband.) Instead, I hoped and I prayed. God answered in ways that went far beyond what I could have anticipated.

What are you hoping for? For what are you turning to your awesome God? Are you longing for a good residency slot? A practice offer in a community that has everything you want and need? Has it been hard to wait? Have you gone through suffering in the process of waiting expectantly? Take heart—God uses even the suffering to produce hope in us. "We also rejoice in our sufferings, because we know that suffering produces perseverance; perseverance, character; and character, hope" (Romans 5:3-4). Remember He is the Author and the Finisher. He knows the end of every story. He uses the difficulties of life as part of the process of building our confidence in His plans for our future. Oh, how marvelous are His ways!

Are you in need of a transfusion of hopefulness in to your anemic life? Has hopelessness instead taken its toll on your body? Claim His promises and encouragement as you reflect on Isaiah 40:29-31: "He gives strength to the weary and increases the power of the weak. Even youths grow tired and weary, and young men stumble and fall; but those who hope in the LORD will renew their strength. They will soar on wings like eagles; they will run and not grow weary, they will walk and not be faint."

Stopping to proclaim my utter dependence on Him for each breath, each day, each circumstance can help me to see the ways He wants to reveal Himself to me. Stopping to remember God's amazing faithfulness—those God stories of my past—indeed brings me to a place of fearful awe of Him. In those moments I have no choice but to say, "He is holy. He is worthy of my reverence, my trust, my hope, and my all."

Rx: Find rest in trusting in God who gives hope even in the hard times.

Chapter 7
The Path of Righteousness

Name :

Address :

Age :

Date :

The ordinances of the LORD are sure and altogether righteous.

—Psalm 19:9b

Label ☐

Refill 0 1 2 3 4 5 PRN

Refill 0 1 2 3 4 5 PRN

Throughout most of my married life with Ed, we have been blessed to live in places of great natural beauty. Often the terrain has been rugged and hilly with ample hiking opportunities, and we love to take advantage of them. Getting lost on the trail has never been our plan, but there have been times when we ended up wandering in circles and feeling a bit nervous about our situation. Thankfully we always managed to find our way back home to safety, to cupboards filled with food, cozy beds, and even the medical supplies needed to tend our scratches and blisters.

Isn't life really a bit like a God-planned hike through fabulous, ever-changing scenery? Sometimes the way is rugged, the path may be hard to see on occasion, and there are times when we wander in confusion. Thankfully, we can always plan on a good ending, though we may need a few band-aids along the way.

God has given us the supreme map and compass for life. With the guidelines He gives in His Word and the Holy Spirit as our perfect leader, we can walk through our days with confidence, knowing He who has made us has a plan for us. And those steps can be sure, unfaltering steps, because we are following the One who is faithful and true and righteous. The word sure, another Hebrew jewel in Psalm 19, means secure, stable, firm, consistent, and reliable. God's Word not only keeps our steps from slipping off the path He has planned for us, but it also reflects who He is—always there, always leading, always right.

Accountable for Myself

I must confess that I often want others around me to be right and just, while I am not as willing to work on this quality in my own life. Do you find yourself wanting your husband to be righteous— especially according to your personal definition of righteousness? Although we are on the journey together, God keeps reminding me that I am accountable to Him for myself, *not* for my husband! A wise older woman once referred to this as "not being his Holy Spirit." How insightful this was for me as I realized I had tried many times to fill this role in my husband's life that is not mine to fill.

Actually, the purpose of the Holy Spirit in each Christian's life is often misunderstood and overlooked. The precious Holy Spirit is a gift, a personal Being, given to each one of us individually when we choose to accept Jesus as Savior and Lord of our life. We have the Holy Spirit to counsel us, to remind us of God's Word and to help us to understand it, to give us His power and contentment in dealing with life, to show us the Father's will, to transform us, and to guide us into all truth (John 14:26; Acts 1:8; Psalm 25:5).

Often we are drawn to God as we observe the behavior of those that know Him and have His Spirit in them. That pull is the Holy Spirit's living fruit at work. First Peter 3:1 says, "Wives, in the same way be submissive to your husbands so that, if any of them do not believe the word, they may be won over without words by the behavior of their wives, when they see the purity and reverence of your lives."

When I became a believer, I really wanted my husband to have the joy of the Lord in his life, like I did. I tried convincing him (being his "Holy Spirit") and used many words to no avail. When a friend shared 1 Peter 3:1 with me, I must admit, I was very skeptical. How could this possibly be effective? But I really wanted to be obedient and this was my opportunity to show God I was serious about my new walk with Him. I began to apply this verse as best I could. To my amazement, God's plan worked! It was the beginning of me truly understanding that His ways are best. Ed became a believer a year after I did and shares in his testimony how my behavior (can you imagine?) won him to the Lord.

Of course, I struggled then and still struggle now to be responsible to God for only my words and actions. It can be quite difficult to remember to focus on pleasing God alone, despite the circumstances that occur around me. Those times when I have done it the right way were when I asked God to enable me to do what pleased Him and honored my husband.

Even when we feel we have been wronged, we must follow Jesus' example. "But if you suffer for doing good and you endure it, this is commendable before God. To this you were called, because Christ suffered for you, leaving you an example, that you should follow in his steps. 'He committed no sin, and no deceit was found in his mouth.' When they hurled their insults at him, he did not retaliate; when he suffered, he made no threats. Instead, he entrusted himself to him who judges justly. He himself bore our sins in his body on the cross, so that we might die to sins and live for righteousness; by his wounds you have been healed" (1 Peter 2:20-24).

We have the power to "die to sins and live for righteousness" because of the Cross and the gift of the Holy Spirit who is alive in us. We can choose to trust God's ways because they are firm and sure. We can meditate on His Word. Did you know that the word for "meditating" in Hebrew means words and thoughts we mutter over and over in our heart? What is your heart muttering?

Are you ready to ask for His help and choose right actions? I have found that I must bite my tongue most of the time and let God work on my inner self so that I will have the "unfading beauty of a quiet and gentle spirit, which is of great worth in God's sight" (1 Peter 3:4).

Jesus gives us the greatest and most perfect example of humbly submitting to God's will as described in Philippians 2:3-8, "Do nothing out of selfish ambition or vain conceit. Rather, in humility value others above yourselves, not looking to your own interests but each of you to the interests of the others. In your relationships with one another, have the same mindset as Christ Jesus: Who, being in very nature God, did not consider equality with God something to be used to his own advantage; rather, he made himself nothing by taking the very nature of a servant, being made in human likeness. And being found in appearance as a man, he humbled himself by becoming obedient to death—even death on a cross!"

Fallout from the Garden

Stubbornly, that self-centered part of me resists the better way and desires my way. That was a fundamental problem way back in the beginning, when things went terribly wrong. In the beginning God, the wise, artful Creator, made male and female with deliberate care. He made them uniquely different—yet amazingly equal to each other and equally fine in His image.

God gave specific instructions to His precious first children. There are clear indications that the man, Adam, was to lead. He was God's appointed "tie breaker." That's always needed in a partnership of two people, isn't it? Unfortunately, Eve stepped ahead and Adam lagged behind when the serpent brought deception into that perfect place. The father of lies misled Eve concerning obedience and the goodness of God. He caused her to doubt God's best plan for relationship with Him and with Adam. And when Satan's temptation was acted upon, that sin forever changed our human existence.

Curses followed for everyone involved—first for Satan, then Eve, and lastly, Adam. God told Eve (and all women that would follow after her) of her consequences in Genesis 3:16: "I will make your pains in childbearing very severe; with painful labor you will give birth to children. Your desire will be for your husband, and he will rule over you."

Many of us can attest to the pain in childbirth being quite real! And most of us, me included, can also attest to the struggle with the rule part. God's original plan was for the marriage to be a harmonious partnership. One of the most painful consequences of the rebellion against God was that woman would now desire to have her husband's position of authority. She would struggle with God's plan for the husband to have the headship in the marriage relationship. We are indeed equal and both created in God's image. Yet our sovereign God has positioned the husband as the head of the home (Ephesians 5:23).

In other places in Scripture, God also tells us as wives to be submissive. That can indeed be a tough pill to swallow. Our culture would see this directive as a curse, yet in God's Word we see that a willingness to serve is the mark of greatness. Jesus told us that if we want to be great in the kingdom, we should be the servant of all. It is still hard though, isn't it? God does not force submission. Serving your husband is voluntary, in obedience to God, for His glory.

God also has some direct words for our spouses, "Husbands, in the same way be considerate as you live with your wives, and treat them with respect as the weaker partner and as heirs with you of the gracious gift of life, so that nothing will hinder your prayers" (1 Peter 3:7). He is to be considerate, respectful of our weaker physical nature, and remember we are equal recipients of God's grace in eternal life. There is no room for egotism or selfishness here. There is even the warning of hindered prayers. God gave quite a difficult challenge to our husbands—yet it is a challenge that we are not responsible to manage for them.

The Beauty of Submission

Amy Carmichael, in *Learning From God,* wrote, "Instead of the word 'submission' . . . I should write acceptance, for more and more, as life goes on, that word opens doors to rooms of infinite peace, and the heart that accepts asks nothing, for it is at rest, and the pilgrim of love does not need a map or chart: I know my road, it leadeth to His heart."

While the value and equality of women are clearly spelled out in Genesis 1:27, when both male and female are proclaimed to be created in His glorious image, our culture has become confused on the issue of submission. The world tells us to look out for ourselves. Many of us have heard all of our lives that we deserve to be on top, to be the big boss. "Sister, you gotta fight for it." "Don't let men put you down." "Don't be a doormat."

How can equality and value and submission coexist? How can it make sense? Only in and through the perfect sacrificial love of Jesus, the servant of all, does it make sense to His children. The world can only watch in disbelief as we live out this oxymoron—as true greatness comes from selfless serving.

A marriage where each person is self-centered is a disaster waiting to happen. If we try to seek what is best for ourselves first and foremost, we deeply hurt one another. God's way is so much better. It is beautiful to see a marriage where each person seeks what is best for the other. It is ironic that in doing so, we receive what is best for us.

Elizabeth Elliot, in *Keep a Quiet Heart,* explains it this way, "A Christian woman, then, in submission to God, recognizes the divinely assigned authority of her husband (he didn't earn it, remember, he received it by appointment!). She then sets about lending her full strength to helping him do what he's supposed to do, be what he's supposed to be—her head. She's trying to make it easier for him to do his job. She seeks to contribute to his purpose, not to scheme how to accomplish her own."

Marriage works wonderfully when both partners fulfill their roles God's way. But it is necessary to remember that we are responsible to God for *only* our part—regardless of what our husbands do. We are to be submissive unless what is asked goes against the Word of God. We can choose to obey out of simple gratitude to God for what He has done in saving us. We can have confidence that God is completely in control of the future. We can know that He is faithful to help us to be the wives He has called us to be.

For many of us, this issue surfaces when we disagree with our husbands about a decision. Optimally, we should be able to amiably discuss the pros and cons while really listening to one another. Sometimes you will come up with a decision together. Sometimes he may feel your idea is better. Sometimes there will simply not be agreement in how to proceed. That is when we need to give our husbands the authority to make the decision, affirming our confidence in him.

This assurance comes from trusting God. Our husbands will make many good decisions, and we need to let them know how much we appreciate those wise choices. Because he is human, he will also make some poor judgments. You can count on that. We can rest assured that God has a plan to teach him even through a poor decision. Therefore, we most assuredly do not need to say, "I told you so" later (though we will most assuredly be tempted to do so). This may require us to humble ourselves—especially those of us who like to be in control of everything.

It has taken me years to sort out and begin to understand this concept of biblical submission. I think I am beginning to grasp how marvelous it is. My home has more joy and peace and love when I diligently apply this principle. I desperately want to encourage you—I wish we could talk face to face and learn from each other. I know you are doing so many things well—trust God to guide you in this crucial area with His truth and in the power of the Holy Spirit. He will surely show you what this looks like in your home. I can promise you that.

The Way of Disgrace and Destruction

We need to pray consistently for God to transform us into women who see humility as God sees it. Ephesians 4:2 tells us, "Be completely humble and gentle; be patient, bearing with one another in love." This quality, which goes hand in hand with submission, is one of strength and dignity, not the "wimpy" view of humility that is portrayed by our culture. In my experience, it takes much more strength and self-control for a woman to be humble than to do what comes naturally and allow pride to get in the way.

This can be a big challenge for medical spouses, because our husbands are often seen as "playing god" when they practice medicine. No other profession gives a person such a feeling of control over matters of life and death. We may feel like our spouse's ego is in the clouds and we need to bring him back down to earth. There is also our inner sinful nature that compels us to want to remind them of how important we are. We want to be acknowledged as the "good woman behind every good man."

In those times when pride rears its ugly head in my life, I have consistently experienced the disgrace warned about in Proverbs 11:2: "When pride comes, then comes disgrace, but with humility comes wisdom." Another verse says, "Pride goes before destruction, a haughty spirit before a fall" (Proverbs 16:18). These verses show us that the *real* weakness is in fact pride, and if left unchecked, it can have a devastating effect. Sometimes it can be hard to recognize this trait in ourselves, but it sure is apparent to those around us. But equally obvious is a humble, submissive spirit. Ah . . . what a sweet fragrance.

Pride often leaves me with my "foot stuck in my mouth." A perfect example of this happened one evening when Ed and I were attending a dinner with other physicians and their wives. I was having a nice discussion with the doctor sitting next to me about the application process to medical school when I remarked that my husband had applied to medical school after just three years of college. He had been accepted by Jefferson Medical School and had also received letters back from several schools suggesting he complete his final year of college and then reapply. Then I mentioned one other school that had also accepted him, but that Ed had decided not to go there because it was a new program and he wanted to wait until they "had worked out all the bugs."

Personal arrogance caused me to share this. I was proud of my husband and, selfishly, wanted to make myself look good too. I then asked the man next to me where he had gone to medical school and his reply was—you guessed it—to the school with the "bugs." To add to my mortification, he had enrolled the very first year of the program. I was so embarrassed and felt like I had damaged this relationship, and my witness—all due to my ugly big-headedness.

How many times have I let vanity talk instead of listening with a humble heart? I pray that you and I will allow His humility to flow though us—allowing us the opportunity to speak with His wisdom. Remember, Psalm 19 confirms to us that the Lord's plan is the only right, sure way.

None of us are alone in our struggle with pride. We read in Matthew 20 that one mother struggled with her pride in the very presence of the Savior. Imagine that! Approaching Jesus, she knelt with the appearance of humility, and she did what most women would do in a heartbeat—she asked the Lord for special privileges and high places of honor for her two sons. Even though her sons were two of His beloved disciples, His response was the same as it is to us today as we seek lofty positions for ourselves, our husbands, or our children.

His loving, but firm words were, "Whoever wants to become great among you must be your servant, and whoever wants to be first must be your slave—just as the Son of Man did not come to be served, but to serve, and to give his life as a ransom for many" (Matthew 20:26-28).

The world cannot understand this. It is only possible to understand this statement with hearts, souls, and minds touched and empowered by our supernatural God, our Creator. Paul understood this. Even as a prisoner for the Lord, he urges us "to live a life worthy of the calling you have received. Be completely humble and gentle; be patient, bearing with one another in love" (Ephesians 4:1-2). This goes against our natural inclination as sinners.

I am so immensely grateful that God's love for me is unconditional, despite my sin! In response to His great love, our hearts should be compelled to sin less and less and love Him more and more. The Old Testament prophet Micah pleaded with the Israelites—and us today as well—to listen to the Lord and respond appropriately to His kindness and love. "He has showed you, O man, what is good. And what does the Lord require of you? To act justly, to love mercy, and to walk humbly with your God" (Micah 6:8).

Who Rules the Roost?

All human beings struggle with humility and submission, and, as women, we are also challenged with the issues surrounding the husband being the head of the home. But as medical spouses, this is exacerbated by the unique position we find ourselves in. It is difficult to go from being the one who is home the majority of the time, making the decisions and being in charge, to allowing our husbands to have that role. He comes home without knowing what has been going on in many different situations and tries to step back into the leadership role. It is tough on both of us to make this transition. Remember that he really doesn't like being gone and feeling out of the loop any more than you like him to be away.

We are very vulnerable to the Enemy's attacks in this sensitive area of appropriately sharing the role of leadership in the home. How important it is to stay alert for Satan's traps and stay focused on God. One wife described it this way: "Satan prowls around waiting to point out to you that 90 percent of the time you are making all the decisions with money, home, and children—and that just isn't fair. During the other 10 percent you wonder how to handle the inevitable 'horning in' when your husband is home. Satan really promotes martyrdom with me." This wise woman knew the Enemy was ready to pounce.

Giving in to Satan's schemes leaves us feeling empty, angry, and discontent. Contrast that with how we feel when we follow God's righteous ways—we walk in peace, harmony, and contentment. God's truths change our thoughts. They change our questions even in the mundane details of life. For example, "Who *has* to take the garbage out?" becomes, "Who *gets* to take the garbage out and be the servant?"

What a privilege we have as women to model Christ in our homes, to be a servant, to be there to encourage our husbands to be all God created them to be, to be the maintainer of the home while he is the provider—both equally important roles in caring for the family. Usually, even if the woman works full time in a demanding job, she is still most likely the one who maintains the home—making it comfortable, thinking about what's for dinner, noticing the laundry needs to be done, and doing the shopping.

Some of us have the amazing opportunity to be home taking care of our children. This job is a blessing as children are a gift from the Lord (Psalm 127:3-5). But like many blessings, they can seem like a burden when our perspective goes awry. When did you last thank your husband for the opportunity to stay home with the children? Does he hear your gratefulness for his efforts to be a good provider or does he hear comments like, "I can't believe all of the demands placed on me because you are not here—I feel like a single parent."

Do you see yourself as your husband's helpmate, as Scripture teaches? Or do you see it the opposite? Do you think of him as your helpmate when he gets home to help you with the dishes, the kids, and projects around the home? Are there some thoughts and actions you need to change?

A woman has a tremendous influence on those in her home. She has a powerful and crucial role. Her choices change lives . . . either positively or negatively. "By wisdom a house is built, and through understanding it is established; through knowledge its rooms are filled with rare and beautiful treasures" (Proverbs 24:3-4). That is the way I want to decorate my home! Don't you?

Build Him Up

Most of us like being married to a decisive, discerning, and confident man. So, what are we doing to assist him in being that man? Are you humbly and gently encouraging your husband to be the leader of your home? Are you sincerely seeking his advice and wisdom on decisions?

One young medical wife spoke with wonder of the time her new husband, having just received her praise, turned to her aglow and said, "I feel so good when you say that you trust my decisions." The power of those simple words and the obvious boost it gave to her husband impacted her deeply.

The problem of limited time together is that it is all too easy to just make decisions while he is gone and inform him of them later with a casual, "By the way . . ." There are many decisions that he does want you to go ahead and handle. However, you need to know which decisions he thinks are yours to handle and which ones he wants you to make together or on his own.

Dialoging about decisions is so helpful to both husband and wife as we can gain so much from each other's perspective. We often make a much better decision with the input of both partners. Wise is the man who listens to his wife in these matters. Wise is the woman who graciously shares her point of view. Wise is the woman who has spent time with her Lord and Master gaining His wisdom first and foremost.

Recently I prayed for and watched the steps of a woman who followed through on this decision-making process so well. The couple had tried for several years to have a baby. When their son was born, the desire of her heart was to be home with their new baby. Because of the financial constraints of Kevin being in residency, he felt that she really needed to continue her full-time job.

Lindsay did her research well and presented a number of issues, in a gracious way: how much child care would cost, how much more they would spend for work clothes, convenience foods, and other expenses if she continued to work full time. She was terribly disappointed when Kevin decided that they still needed the income from her full-time job. Lindsay submitted to his decision despite her torn heart and sought God in prayer.

A difficult year followed where she did her best to juggle her job and the needs of her family. A new decision-making point came when the childcare provider could no longer care for their son. This was a circumstance that Lindsay saw as being from the Lord. Kevin had seen how hard the past year had been on his wife and together they decided to have her leave her job and stay home with their son by being more creative with their finances.

Now they are a much happier and healthier family. Lindsay is thoroughly enjoying her time raising her son and efficiently running her home. An added benefit has been more time together and much better communication with her husband. They have also seen God provide for their finances as they continue to depend on Him. Today Lindsay is reaping the rewards of accepting her husband's decision and trusting God to bring to fruition the desires of her heart. But she feels the best part is what she learned during that year, as she kept her focus on God through the difficulties and allowed Him to refine her.

While it would be wonderful if we were always on the same page, sometimes a decision needs to be made and you are not in agreement about what to do. This is when we are called to allow our husbands to make the decision as head of the home, as Lindsay did so well. Someone has to make the final decision, and God has appointed our husbands to be the one. He will make good decisions often, and you will be blessed as a result. He will make poor ones at times, and God will teach him from those, too—especially if we get out of the way.

How blessed is the man who is encouraged to be who God has called him to be in the home. How blessed is a home where the man is the spiritual leader. A friend, laughingly but quite seriously, said the biggest "turn on" for her for sexual intimacy with her husband was when he took the leadership role in their home—especially in the spiritual realm. Other women present agreed that this was at the top of their lists of qualities that they desired their husband to have.

For many years I was frustrated with Ed concerning his not taking the lead with spiritual matters like family devotion time. I felt like this was one more thing I did in our home that was really his job. It wasn't until I prayed about it and went to Ed with a right heart (I had to pray awhile for the right heart part to come!) that I understood what the problem was. He saw me already fulfilling this role and, in his opinion, doing it well, so why should he attempt it and possibly fail?

I had no idea that this was how he perceived things. But after our discussion, Ed did begin to assume his rightful place and truly became a godly spiritual leader in our home. Isn't it just like God to answer this prayer, consistent with His will, beyond my greatest expectations?

It is true that our husbands are gone a lot, but if we look for opportunities to encourage them in their God-given role, we will find plenty. Simple questions and suggestions can bring about much spiritual fruit in our homes, such as, "Would you like to pray for us in this matter or would you like me to?" "Would you like to read the Bible story to the children tonight or would it be helpful to you if I did?" "There is an event at the church that I am interested in attending. How do you feel about it?" "I really appreciate the godly wisdom you showed in that decision. I'm so proud of you."

Join me in praying that God will help us to see things His way. Pray that we will remember Christ's servant-hearted example and imitate Him. Pray that we will be mindful of all the mighty and marvelous things He has done for us. Pray that we will trust Him for everything in our lives—and that love would be our motivation to follow His ordinances.

Through relationship with Christ we can know Him, have salvation, be forgiven, become His daughters, and be given truth and the power of His Spirit to live it out. To top it all off, we get to live with Him forever! "Praise be to the God and Father of our Lord Jesus Christ, who has blessed us in the heavenly realms with every spiritual blessing in Christ" (Ephesians 1:3).

I really love the words "heavenly realms" from that verse. They remind me that blessings are eternal and that they are spiritual. They are not of this world. God is reminding us to rise above what is happening around us on this earth—to focus instead on the higher spiritual aspects of our lives. His sure and righteous pathways here lead us to the glory of heaven.

We are promised security and clear godly ways through God's instructions. Moses received these promises, too, long before us. He was used by God to remind the Israelites, "Acknowledge and take to heart this day that the LORD is God in heaven above and on earth below. There is no other. Keep his decrees and commands, which I am giving you today, so that it may go well with you" (Deuteronomy 4:39-40). Sure-footedness was God's plan for His children then and still is for us today.

God's loving decrees are indeed righteous, laying the straight path and keeping each of us from stumbling and going in crazy circles. They are sure—absolutely true, certain, secure, and firm. Marvel at them. Delight in following them with great confidence in your marriage, in your friendships, as a mother, and with every step you take on life's pathways.

Rx: Follow God as He leads, and remember to be accountable to God for you alone.

Chapter 8

R̲X̲

True Friends and Lovers

Name :   Age :

Address :   Date :

They are more precious than gold, than much pure gold; they are sweeter than honey, than honey from the honeycomb.

—Psalm 19:10

Label ☐

Refill 0 1 2 3 4 5 PRN

Refill 0 1 2 3 4 5 PRN

The water supply for the lake we live on is provided, in part, by Contrary Creek. The fascinating history of this little stream goes back generations, to the gold-rush years when that most highly sought-after precious metal was found here. Like many other sites around the country, a town sprang up rapidly nearby as countless people came to this little creek from far and wide, hoping to make their fortunes. People still pan for gold there today, eagerly seeking nuggets of this precious substance and secretly hoping to find enough to make them instantly wealthy.

We inherently understand the value of this precious metal and its connection to great wealth. Scripture uses this metaphor of gold to help us understand how valuable the inspired Word of God is. His Word is more prized than gold—to be treasured more than any vast, unlimited wealth. It is of far greater worth than anything man strives for in this world. Much like the fortune-seekers of the gold rush era, the psalmist invites us to mine for the precious treasures found in the pages of this Book.

In the same way, God's Word is more valuable than any fine food—the "sweet honey" man continually searches for. The Holy

Spirit beckons us to taste the finest truths found in God's love letter to us. The real story of God's love demonstrated through Jesus' sacrifice for us is the most magnificent of all. This image is lived out for the world to see in the love between a husband and a wife. If God is the center of a marriage, then He is glorified. If self is at the center, then much heartache occurs and God's image is hard to see.

Sadly, the world yearns for the real gold of God, but settles for a counterfeit. They fill their growling stomachs with feasts of false love. What about us? Are we truly enjoying the real deal? Let's dig for His gold that supplies riches beyond compare. Let's satisfy our taste buds with His delicacies beyond description. Let's "taste and see that the LORD is good" (Psalm 34:8).

Love and Longing

Many weddings include the well-known passage from 1 Corinthians 13:4-8, "Love is patient, love is kind. It does not envy, it does not boast, it is not proud. It is not rude, it is not self-seeking, it is not easily angered, it keeps no record of wrongs. Love does not delight in evil but rejoices with the truth. It always protects, always trusts, always hopes, always perseveres. Love never fails."

These words are indeed "sweeter than honey" and possessing them in your marriage is "more precious than gold." Who wouldn't want this in their home? We all start off believing that our marriage will have all of these qualities and more. And while many couples continue to grow into a deeper and more fulfilling love, other couples seem to grow apart, disregarding the wise instruction of these words.

How do you see your marriage now? Are you tired of trying to convince yourself that all is fine? Are you feeling hopeless that what you thought might just be a "phase" or a "season of life" may be a constant reality? Is your soul weary from the struggle? Are you feeling alone? Frustrated? Forgotten? If so, be encouraged, for these needs will lead you to the Great Physician. Jesus proclaimed that He came for the sick, not those who are well. Take heart, dear friend. Hang in there. We have all been there. Let God do a heart transplant—replacing your sorrow and emptiness of heart with His strength and joy.

It is so hard to focus on God and His Word when we are struggling. What we need the most seems the hardest to do in those times. Don't stay stuck. When you struggle to think of even one Bible verse that might lift you out of the gloom and give you hope, I encourage you to recall the verses that Jesus told us were the greatest commandments. "Jesus replied, 'Love the Lord your God with all your heart and all your soul and with all your mind. This is the first and greatest commandment. And the second is like it: Love your neighbor as yourself'" (Matthew 22:37-39).

An initial heart check is needed to see where we are in our relationship with our heavenly Bridegroom. The imagery of a bridegroom and his bride is some of the most striking used in Scripture to describe our tender, intimate closeness with God. He lovingly calls to us. We are drawn to desire to love Him in return. Out of that love comes an aspiration to love other people.

Love is the greatest entity there is. Nothing else compares. We desperately desire to receive it. We wholeheartedly need to give it. We know this and yet somehow we forget to love each other. We neglect loving God with all of our being; with everything that we have. Easily distracted, we lose sight of the need to embrace God's love for us and to then be a conduit of His love to others around us—especially to the mate He has given us.

One of my favorite passages in Scripture is in John 15:1-17, where Jesus describes Himself as the true vine, God as the gardener, and us as the branches. He challenges us in verse 5 with our need to remain in Him in order to produce fruit and that "apart from [Him] we can do nothing." Nothing! Jesus then tells us to remain in His love so that our "joy may be complete." Finally, He commands us to "love each other as I have loved you" and says that we "are my friends if you do what I command." There is so much truth to digest and dissect in this wonderful passage about love and friendship. God loves us and loves others through us as we abide in him. We are told to love others and that the source of our love is God's amazing sacrificial love for us.

The Value of Friendship

None of us wants to drift apart in our relationship with our husband. How can we purposely do our best to avoid this? We need to prevent deep wounds by caring for each other's hearts before an injury happens. But once a wound does occur, we don't want a band-aid to do a temporary fix, we need to call upon the Great Physician to bring His healing hand to repair the damage. We can't wait too long or the patient will no longer have a detectable heartbeat.

Loneliness is a common malady in a medical marriage. Often our husbands are absent for long hours, leaving us with too much time alone. Attending events and functions by yourself can be so hard that you find yourself just staying home—leading to even more loneliness. We can, and sometimes do, wallow in this misery. For those medical wives who are on the medical mission field, the isolation and loneliness can be even more devastating.

The key is not to stay in this dangerous state. Cling to your best friend, Jesus, who is always there. Find friends to spend time with from all different walks of life. Find a Side by Side group to fellowship with other women who understand your life and can encourage you.

Be "a friend [that] loves at all times" (Proverbs 17:17) to others who also need a friend.

Most importantly, be a friend to your husband. We are often unaware that he may be truly lonely. He may even be unaware of this himself or simply too busy to address his need for relationships.

In their online column *Marriage Minutes,* authors and conference speakers Bob and Cheryl Moeller, share some interesting information concerning men's unique need for friendship.

> While a wife might believe the loneliest man she knows is a widower or a single male, it very well could be her husband.
>
> In Genesis God looks at Adam and says, "It's not good that man be alone." This was before sin had entered the world—so his loneliness and desire for a companion were part of God's design. When women lose their husbands, 75 percent of them never remarry, but when a man loses his wife 80 percent remarry.
>
> Studies show that most American men say they do not have one close friend—in other words they are lonely. Wise is the wife who chooses to be her husband's friend—even buddy—she will be meeting one of his deepest needs. Men need shoulder-to-shoulder communication rather than face-to-face communication. . . . A survey of 400 divorced men said the number one trait they admired and wanted in their next wife was, "to be my best friend."

How would you describe your relationship with your husband? Is he your best friend? Would he consider you to be his best friend?

What are you doing to build your friendship? We crave this deep companionship with our spouse. But often, we are confused as to how we can have this special closeness in our relationship.

In his book *Love and Respect,* Emerson Eggerichs describes his concept of the "shoulder-to-shoulder friendship" that our husbands desire. "This is how men communicate, by sharing experiences. Women share experiences by talking about them to each other, examining and infusing the experience with their impressions and emotions. Men are different. They share their experiences by sharing an activity. This is what your husband wants to do with you."

You can probably picture the tension. You long for a romantic dinner gazing into one another's eyes and talking about what is going on in your lives and in your hearts. He wants you to sit next to him and watch a movie or kayak with him or take a hike together or anything that means limited words and just time spent next to each other.

It is crucial that we understand each other's differences and seek to meet one another's needs. There is a mutual need for many things as well, such as kind words. We have already established that God's Word is sweeter than honey. Proverbs 16:24 reminds us that, "Pleasant words are a honeycomb, sweet to the soul and healing to the bones." Our words have such power to build up or tear down our dear husbands.

Think about how he would describe your way of relating to him. Are your words sweet? Is your attitude respectful? Are you kind to him? Affirming? Do you cover small offenses with grace? Do you overlook his faults and focus on his positive qualities? Do you seek to be someone he really wants to spend time with? What kind of companion does he find fun to be around? Are you that kind of person?

"A friend loves at all times" is wise advice from Proverbs 17:17. Of course, we want to be loved—no matter what. Do we extend that unconditional love in return? Take a moment to read through 1 Corinthians 13 and test yourself. What characteristics of love do you display? Which ones do you need to work on?

Genesis 2:24 points to an important "gold nugget" concerning marriage, "For this reason a man will leave his father and mother and be united to his wife, and they will become one flesh." We are reminded that in marriage, we now form an inseparable union. We are bonded in a profound oneness, both physically and spiritually. We need to guard this oneness and not allow family members to come between us. Leaving family and cleaving to one another are crucial in a deep friendship with our man and in building precious intimacy.

Do what you can to build the intimate relationship you desire. Be open and honest about your needs and wishes as well. It is amazing how aware he will become of your needs if you truly seek to meet his. (Remember, even if he doesn't become more aware of your needs, you have pleased God, and that is motivation enough!)

The Bible gives us a great example of how to grow a loving friendship. "Don't just pretend to love others. Really love them. Hate what is wrong. Hold tightly to what is good. Love each other with genuine affection, and take delight in honoring each other" (Romans 12:9-10 NLT). This is an active love, not one that passively dreams of a relationship getting better.

A few verses later we are given a great formula against apathy, "Be joyful in hope, patient in affliction, faithful in prayer" (Romans 12:12). In other words—don't stay stuck. Start today—with God's help and the encouragement of sisters in Christ—to become best friends with your husband.

The Joy of Intimacy

The Bible uses some pretty steamy phrasing describing this intimate friendship in Song of Songs 5:16 where it declares, "His mouth is sweetness itself; he is altogether lovely. This is my beloved, this is my friend," Whew! Try thinking about and then believing those words!

Limited time together and sensitivity to gender differences can make sexual intimacy in a medical marriage a real challenge! Of course, everyone assumes that the doctor has all the answers on this subject. After all, isn't this one of the primary issues that patients ask their physicians about?

I can't help but smile as I recall the struggles Ed and I had after being newly married. Since we were married three days before medical school began and two years into the four years of my BS in nursing school, we knew very little about this complicated subject. Yet, we were a doctor and nurse who were supposed to know all about human sexuality. Unfortunately there was no one to consult. No parents open to discussing this subject, no premarital counseling to draw on, no mentors to consult, and no books that we knew of on the topic. So, where does a good medical student go for help? He goes to the medical library and copies articles (now we can look up the subject on our computers) that might help us with our area of confusion. Unfortunately, those articles were only minimally helpful.

How very thankful we are that the subject is now discussed in pre-marital counseling, among couples that mentor, and in some wonderful, godly books that are available today. There are other resources you can draw on as well. For example, deliberately seek out older women on this topic, putting aside any embarrassment. We need each other. One wise mentor, in addressing intimacy, said to a younger woman about to be married, "Let me give you one bit of advice. Just remember it is not like the movies!" The young woman has mentioned that statement many times as a great reality check and personal help.

In Les and Leslie Parrott's book *Saving Your Marriage Before It Starts*, they write, "Every successful marriage is the result of two people working together diligently and skillfully to cultivate their love." They discuss building a marriage based on the full combination of love's three components: passion, intimacy, and commitment. In cultivating intimacy, they explain several areas that are important. One of them is to spend time together. They quote marriage expert David Mace who says, "Love must be fed and nurtured . . . first and foremost it demands time." I believe you and I would say a hearty *amen* to that.

The reality is we do not have the time together that we need because there are too many demands already on our husband's time. So, what are we to do? Over and over again it is clear that we need the Lord's help. "Is anything too hard for God?" (Genesis 18:14 msg). I am encouraged and impacted by the words of Linda Dillow when she says, "God is alive and well today! He is not just an abstract theory, but a living person who actually invades lives and changes situations."

It is so important to remember that you are in a marriage that is constantly changing. Gary Chapman, in his book *The Four Seasons of Marriage*, writes:

> Marriages are in a perpetual state of transition, continually moving from one season to another—perhaps not annually, as in nature, but certainly and consistently. Sometimes we find ourselves in Winter—distant, discouraged, and dissatisfied; other times we experience

Springtime—filled with hope, openness, and anticipation. Sometimes we bask in the warmth of Summer—satisfied and comfortable, simply enjoying life together. In times of Fall, negligence and uncertainty creep in, leaving us feeling unsettled and apprehensive.

The cycle repeats itself many times throughout the life of a marriage, just as the seasons repeat themselves in nature. Each season presents its own unique challenges, and each holds the potential for emotional health and happiness. The purpose of [this] book is to help you and your spouse identify which season your marriage is currently in, give you a common language with which to discuss your marriage, and provide practical strategies that will help you strengthen and enhance your relationship.

Your marriage will change through the seasons, but it also changes throughout the years as you spend your life together. Keep in mind that you are building upon a foundation that you want to stand the test of time. Do what you can now to spend time wisely with your husband—talking, sharing, listening, laughing, and playing. He will not always spend so many hours away. His schedule will not always be so overwhelming to him and to you.

You want to have assembled moments in the day-to-day of life that will flourish when the time comes that you will have a lot more time together. You don't want to look across the dinner table when the children have left the nest or your job ends or he retires and find you have nothing in common and are wondering how to relate as "strangers." It is well worth the effort to tenderly care for all aspects of your marriage now. God will surely help us. Psalm 4:3 gives us confidence, "the LORD will hear when I call to him."

Sex Changes Everything

Recently I met with my beloved group of Side by Side women where we discussed the topic of sex. It was a lively discussion, as you can imagine. Our subject matter for the evening was chapter five of Shaunti Feldhahn's book *For Women Only* entitled "Sex Changes Everything." All of the women were married to a medical student, a resident, or a physician, and they had a lot to say about the subject. All of us were struck with the words on page 92: "In a very deep way, your man often feels isolated and burdened by secret feelings of inadequacy. Making love with you assures him that you find him desirable, salves a deep sense of loneliness, and gives him the strength and well-being necessary to face the world with confidence. And, of course, sex also makes him feel loved—in fact, he can't feel completely loved without it."

Several women were surprised to learn of the emotional need in their husbands and that sex was not just a physical need. Feldhahn went on to state that "lack of sex is as emotionally serious to him as, say, his sudden silence would be to you, were he to simply stop communicating with you." Wow . . . this had the attention of the group. They began to express that having little time together left them feeling emotionally disconnected from their husbands. Now they realized that they wanted time together and good communication to connect emotionally with him *before* sex, while he needed sex to meet his emotional need so that he was ready to meet her needs *after*. Talk about a set up for disaster! What are we to do?

The most important thing we can do is go directly to God's Word. Our group continued to discuss what He had to say in this area. Verses such as 1 Corinthians 7:5 reminded us that it is *not* about us: "Do not deprive each other except by mutual consent and for a time, so that you may devote yourselves to prayer. Then come together again so that Satan will not tempt you because of your lack of self-control." We are not to deprive him because our need is not met. This does not mean we shouldn't discuss our own needs and desires. But it does mean that we should seek first what pleases the Lord and then what pleases our husbands. This does not mean that there are not appropriate times and reasons to avoid sex, but these need to be agreed on mutually.

Philippians 2:4-8 says, "Each of you should look not only to your own interests, but also to the interests of others. Your attitude should be the same as that of Christ Jesus: Who, being in very nature God, did not consider equality with God something to be grasped, but made himself nothing, taking the very nature of a servant, being made in human likeness." We have a chance to imitate Christ as we look to the needs of our husbands instead of our own.

We shouldn't be motivated by a reward, but God often blesses our efforts in doing things His way. We may find that our husband desires to meet our emotional and physical needs in a much deeper way as he senses our desire to meet his physical and emotional needs. Of course, it is even better if we also initiate and respond to him sexually—not just make love out of a sense of duty with no real investment of ourselves in the relationship.

Practical Advice

Let's go back to that issue of insufficient time together. How do we handle this problem so that it does not come between us when it comes to sexual intimacy? One woman suggested writing possible times on her calendar and being ready in creative ways to meet his need. This helped her to be prepared, and she said he was "happy" to have her initiate. This young woman certainly has the right idea.

A book published in the early 1970s, called *The Total Woman*, suggested meeting your husband at the door wrapped in only saran wrap. That doesn't sound like a good idea to me, but planning ahead sure is.

Kevin Lehman's book entitled *Sex Begins in the Kitchen* was always a favorite to mention to my busy husband in the early years of our marriage. I loved the idea that it was his job to set up our bedroom time through sweet moments of helping and connecting in the kitchen—complete with romantically whispered words. Ah, what a dream. In principle that idea is a true and worthy goal, yet how impossible it seems at times for our men with their grueling schedules.

More often than not, I have learned that sex really begins when I direct my concentrated attention on my husband and focus on our physical intimacy time just around the corner. This includes my letting go of the day's menu, the carpooling needs, the laundry pile, my responsibility concerning the church potluck—all cares for that matter.

Pastor Robert Lewis, author of *Rocking the Roles,* once explained to a mixed church group that while wives could hear the refrigerator door open at the neighbor's house in the middle of sex, a man would be completely unaware that a train had run off the tracks and was barreling through the bedroom. How true. God can help us with our ears and our minds as we lie in our husband's arms or prepare for what can be a blissful time for both.

Wisely, Kevin Lehman points out, "All it takes is practice . . . and the right attitude . . . sex is about the quality of your entire life, not just the alignment of your bodies." He also wrote, "Sexual intimacy is an expression of the care you and your spouse show each other in all areas of life—in communicating, in sharing thoughts and feelings, and even in helping out around the house." Don't you agree?

Many women have mentioned to me that it can be very frustrating for them when they are interested in sexual intimacy, but their husband is not. They long for that connection and he sees it as one more demand. It sure is hard to keep from feeling rejected and responding in anger. Our prayers may be different in this particular circumstance, but the principles that need to be applied are the same as those we have been gleaning from God's Word in other situations.

Occasionally, the times when our husbands are interested and available for intimacy are frankly not convenient or conducive to exciting our passion. Many of our husbands keep strange hours. They might be delivering a baby in the middle of the night, as my husband often did when he practiced family medicine. It wasn't much better when he practiced emergency medicine and had unusual shifts.

I recall quite a few times when he would be interested at bedtime—but his bedtime was 3:00 a.m., and I was barely conscious when he crawled into bed. I certainly was not thinking about much except getting back to sleep. At those times, I was especially thankful that God is always awake and available to talk to. And yes, God cares about sex—after all, He created it! I was amazed many times how God answered my prayers to allow me to be interested and to respond to my husband. He was satisfied, and I was able to sleep contentedly in his arms. So much better than my original thought: *It's 3:00 a.m., he can't be serious!*

Resist being tainted by the views our world has of sex—perverted by selfishness and exploitation. How captivating it is to see the godly model of a marriage based on love and commitment! God can help us have that kind of marriage. You can have a union that honors Him, despite what was modeled to you in your home of origin or in the current culture around you.

Guard Your Marriage

It is worth mentioning that many women likely find your husband desirable. Does your husband know that *you* find him desirable? That no man on earth can please you like him? Do you tell him? Do you show him? Does he really feel it in his terms?

At the hospital, he is respected, wealthy (only we are aware of the huge debt), smart, compassionate, and handsome. Lots of women—both co-workers and patients—will have eyes for him. Be aware and proactive in protecting your marriage. I know an older doctor and his wife who regularly made a point of walking together through the hospital corridors while holding hands, basically proclaiming, "Hear ye! Hear ye! We love each other!"

Make sure as best you can that he only has eyes for you. What does he like for you to wear? What do you wear around his colleagues that makes him feel proud—eager to have his arm around you? What is pleasing to his eyes when it is just the two of you? What does he find sexy? What music does he like? How does he like you to smell?

In fact, do you give off a sweet inner fragrance? Now, that is sexy! That is inviting! First Peter 3:3 encourages wives, "Your beauty should not be from outward adornment, such as braided hair and the wearing of gold jewelry and fine clothes. Instead, it should be that of . . . a gentle and quiet spirit, which is of great worth in God's sight." This doesn't mean we should not focus on how we look, but this ought not be our only focus. Beauty radiating from within is much more appealing.

It is important to talk about some very practical things as far as sexual intimacy is concerned. A healthy body image is always key in the subject of sexuality. God has made us in all different shapes and sizes. Never forget that. Many wives battle the bulge in the childbearing years—or maybe their whole life long. Or possibly you find yourself in the "less endowed" category. We must not . . . we cannot . . . allow ourselves to be dismayed by how we compare to the world's definition of sexual beauty. Instead, as best you can, be in good physical shape—whatever shape God has assigned you. Don't waste your energy trying to be something you are not.

Exercise, healthy eating, and ample rest (wise advice often given by our doctor husbands to their patients) will rarely let you down. Feeling good about your physical condition and efforts to stay healthy will be a personal, as well as sexual, boost. In addition, you will be caring for your body, which is a temple of the Holy Spirit (see 1 Corinthians 6:19).

Another wise piece of advice is to avoid falling into the dreaded state of frumpiness. A healthy, cheerful woman, yet one who is always dressed in sweats and t-shirts might not be your husband's favorite sight upon coming home. Don't feel as though you have to be a slave to fashion, but try keeping track of what he will see "out here" that can also look lovely on you. Your goal may not be the height of fashion, but you can be appropriately fashionable and feminine, not frumpy!

A wise woman seeks to meet the needs of her husband with the Lord's help. She looks for opportunities to build her home by assessing her relationship with *the* Bridegroom, and then building her relationship with the husband with whom God has blessed her. She is to be his committed friend—closer than all others, and his lover—growing ever more intimate.

Trust, security, history with each other—all these things make bedroom intimacy better and sweeter. Be assured that who you are as a newlywed is not who you will be after thirty years of marriage. I have to say that intimacy now, after many years of marriage, is much better than my memories of the honeymoon. My husband agrees. Seek to continually grow sexually as a wife, as a helpmate.

Our glitzy, self-focused world, with its warped view of sexiness and beauty will not be able to understand. But your God-centered, God-fueled marriage can be one that is as precious as pure gold and sweeter than fine honey.

Rx: Enjoy the benefits of enhancing your relationship as friend and lover to your husband.

Chapter 9

Rx

Strength for the Storm

Name :

Age :

Address :

Date :

By them is your servant warned; in keeping them there is great reward.

—Psalm 19:11

Label ☐

Refill 0 1 2 3 4 5 PRN

Refill 0 1 2

t is wonderful, in this season of my life, to have more time to spend with my dear husband. Whether doing chores or simply having fun together, I appreciate the hours with him very much after so many years of limited time. Not long ago, Ed and I were doing some yard work. He was cutting the grass, while I was weeding and sweeping. Out of the corner of my eye, I saw an unexpected wildflower blooming along the edge of the woods. Of course, I stopped what I was doing in order to go and inspect this wonder more closely.

I was delighted to find a gorgeous, morning glory type of white flower with a lovely lilac center. This vine-like plant had multiple perfect blooms and buds. I began to thank God for this beautiful creation. I marveled at His ability to cause such a stunning flower to grow in a dark, dry, rocky, and barren place. Remarkably, this flower was more striking than many in my garden that I fertilized, watered, and cared for.

With tears, I thanked God for this reminder—given just for me—of His provision for *all* of His creation. He will enable me to flourish despite the "rocky" places I find myself in at times. He will sustain me and enable me to grow as He nourishes me. He will allow me to bloom with natural beauty as He changes me through the dark times in life.

A wise woman willingly commits herself to God's will. He promises amazing rewards to the one who keeps on the right path—which is often the narrow one. There may be stubborn "rocks" and desert-like "dry" times, but the Father is tenderly caring for her every need along the way. She is directed to hidden treasures along life's journey to be carefully excavated, inspected, polished, and displayed. Compensation for this diligent work includes the God-given blessings of joy, wisdom, and contentment.

God's Word will transform me, and you, to the extent we allow it to. It will make us beautiful for God and to others. His Word prepares us for life and the hazards that lie on the road ahead with a heaven-sent flashing yellow light. The godly woman who heeds His caution is forewarned of possible dangers. She is shown the places to firmly place her feet as she walks through the obstacles of life.

Innumerable are the benefits of wholeheartedly following God. The treasures you store up will make a huge difference in this life and in the next. One of those rewards is a relationship built with your life partner that stands strong upon a firm foundation—the Rock.

When the Unthinkable Happens

Not everything goes exactly the way we expect it to. This chapter was not planned when I began to write this book. At least, not by me. It was known only by our heavenly Father. But I believe God has supernaturally given me a new understanding of His truth to share with you.

Something unthinkable and unimaginable has happened in my life. As a result, I have been dramatically changed through a life experience that cements in my mind and heart the primary need for a vibrant relationship with God and my secondary need for a strong relationship with my husband. The words to describe the dreadful events come with tears and a heavy heart. But I will try to find a way to share this heartbreaking story with you as I cling tightly to Him.

When I first began this project, I set aside time to write each day. At the time, my schedule was a little lighter than usual, which gave me the perfect opportunity to discipline myself to work each morning, writing and rewriting what I felt led to share with you. That left the rest of the day for relationship building, work, and the many tasks that always seemed to be waiting.

A sweet family reunion had just ended at our home with many delightful memories made. Two days later, on this particular Tuesday, I remember praying and asking God to guide my words and thoughts as I prepared to write. My life forever changed within those next few hours.

It was a lovely morning. A rare summer day—the sun was shining and the temperature was very pleasant. As I glanced out the window, I could see our son, Jon, down at the dock of our home by the lake. He was living with us for a few months while waiting to begin graduate school in August. He had been laid off from his job were he worked with troubled kids in a wilderness therapy program. The economy had affected enrollment and several people were asked to leave.

The timing seemed right for Jon to pursue his master's degree in watershed stewardship to build upon his undergraduate environmental biology degree. His desire was to help provide wells to communities in foreign lands as a means to also spread the Gospel. Ever since our mission trip to El Salvador where he first learned of this great need, the vision of providing clean water and sharing about the Living Water of Jesus really excited him. Only one school had the program he really wanted. God further paved the way by allowing Jon to be accepted there.

In May, Jon came home to live with us and work for us during the summer months. The long list of spring chores included mulching, mowing, and power washing. He was a huge help, and I loved working beside him. We shared a love of the beauty of God's creation—especially birds, flowers, and mountains. Together, on the previous Sunday, we had walked around the yard admiring flowers as he photographed them. I did not have shoes on, so Jon gave me a "piggyback" ride across the driveway that left us both laughing. That was the kind of joy in life that we shared. He was the kind of son that mothers dream of—I was so blessed and so very proud of him.

Jon was struggling that day. I could tell by his constant pacing. The neurological symptoms of Lyme disease made him irritable and restless at times. His symptoms seemed to increase despite the an-tibiotic treatment he had undergone. Often, he would share his struggles, and I would pray for him. He was concerned about how these symptoms might affect his ability to concentrate on his studies at Colorado State. As a bright and capable student, this was a new concern for him.

My mother's heart led me down to the dock to see how he was doing. Jon said he was having a hard day and felt "bored and lonely." Ed and I had been encouraging him to either visit his best friend, Matt, or invite him to our home. Matt was a wonderful young man who shared both Jon's love for God and an adventurous spirit. They had been close friends since being involved together for The Navi-gators ministry at Penn State. Together they had hiked, climbed mountains, sky dived, backpacked, laughed, talked, and prayed. Matt had previously been to our home, and Jon was planning to text him and invite him to visit again. We discussed other ideas that might help. Jon left for the house, assuring me he was "okay." My heart ached to see his struggle, so I did what we as mothers do continually—I went to our heavenly Father in prayer for him.

He came back out to tell me he had booked a train to visit Matt. (He never made a reservation—an unusual claim for Jon who did not have a habit of lying.) He did text Matt to ask about a visit. He e-mailed another college Bible study friend who was already at Colorado State to ask for help in finding an apartment for grad school.

Jon also sent an e-mail to a friend of our niece's telling her about the symptoms of Lyme disease with the suggestion that she be tested. (She was later found to be positive for the disease.) He described how difficult it was to diagnose what was wrong with him—it had taken years—and how the antibiotic treatment had helped him some. That day he wrote, "I feel way better now physically, mentally, emotionally, and spiritually than I did two years ago. Recently, I began to have some horrible headaches, numbness in my arms, and nightmares causing me to lose sleep due to the neurological symptoms of the disease."

Later, that "unsettled" feeling came upon me, often used by the Holy Spirit to draw me to prayer. As I set aside my work on the book and prayed fervently for him again, little did I know how much my precious Jon needed those prayers.

A short time later I found him. Our precious son was dead. Never have I known such anguish and despair. I cried out to God—pleading with Him to turn back time and change this outcome, to miraculously resurrect Jon, or to wake me from this awful nightmare. As we later reconstructed the pieces and events of that day, we believe Jon suddenly lost touch with reality. He had ended his life.

The Rewards of Relationship

I had been there rejoicing when Jon breathed his first breath. I was the first to hold him in my arms, wearing a smile of contentment as evidence of my joy and thankfulness for this precious gift from the Lord. How could it be possible that I was there with him now, clinging to him in grief when he gasped his last breath? The tragedy was unthinkable, the grief almost unbearable, the pain endured unimaginable, the loss was beyond words. We deeply loved Jon—our hearts were broken beyond description.

Ed and I wrote the following ministry newsletter one week later. I am sharing it with you to give you a small glimpse into the life of our dear Jon and our immeasurable grief at the time.

Let us hold unswervingly to the hope we profess,
for he who promised is faithful.
—Hebrews 10:23

We would like to dedicate this newsletter to our beloved son, Jonathan, who left this world on Tuesday, June 23, for his eternal home. Though the loss of our precious son has caused great sorrow beyond words, God has given us much to be thankful for in the midst of this pain. Knowing Jon is with Jesus, whom he loved and trusted in, has given us much comfort. Jon is at peace and free from the suffering of the mental, physical, spiritual, and emotional effects of Lyme disease that tormented him more than we knew. We know we can go on because this same Lord loves us and will carry us through our grief. We know we will be with Jon again in heaven when God calls us home.

The honor of being chosen by God to be Jon's parents . . . to have the privilege of raising him, loving him, and spending time with him . . . was a gift from the Lord. We have loved him dearly and been extremely proud of him. Jon had such a special way about him. He loved people and truly cared about them and desired to get to know them in an authentic way. He was a deep thinker who often had profound things to say. He had a great love for God's creation and enjoyed so many things outdoors. He was an avid mountain climber who was also captivated by reading a classic novel. He loved his family and friends. He cherished time with them. He openly expressed his love through wonderful hugs and sincere words. He was intelligent, thoughtful, and compassionate—we could go on for hours with all the traits that made him so special.

We treasure the gift of time with him over the years that has filled our lives with sweet memories. God gave us the opportunity to have him live with us this summer before he was to start grad school at Colorado State in August. He gave us many precious moments with Jon such as him playing his guitar for us and singing songs he had written, having deep spiritual discussions, and enjoying fun at the lake together.

We are overwhelmed and greatly encouraged by the outpouring of love from you and so many others. We are deeply touched by the countless ways you have ministered to us and to our family at this tragic time. God has shown us His great love through you. Your kind words, and your hugs, your prayers on our behalf (now and in the future) are helping us to walk through this time. We are not alone as God, our dear family, and dear friends are beside us as we face the difficult days ahead.

Jon has taught us much about life and love. He packed more into his twenty-seven years than most people do into a long lifetime. Jon impacted many lives in a profound way—especially his adopted brothers and the troubled youth he worked with in Wilderness Therapy. Jon lived life well and loved well. He lived his life in a way that helped teach us that the most important thing in life is relationships—with God and with the family and friends that he deeply loved. One of his favorite books of the Bible was Hosea where Jon was touched by God's intimate love for him. This was reflected in a journal entry where Jon spoke of how awed he was that God didn't need him, but yet still wanted an intimate relationship with him.

This reminder helps us to go forward with what God has called us to do with renewed commitment and sense of purpose. Our desire is to be involved in leading others to know, love, and serve Christ, and to encourage those that know Him already to live wholeheartedly for Him. We want to build new relationships while making stronger relationships with those we already know and love. We want to serve God for His glory and to know Him more intimately.

Thank you for your continued prayers. Please pray for us as we ask God to bring much good from this tragedy that we may use in the lives He will allow us to impact. New residents and students arrive these next two months.

Current residents, students, and practicing doctors are in need of encouragement and focus on God. We covet your prayers as we partner with you in being involved in relationships in a way that truly matters.

Assured of His everlasting love that will heal our broken hearts,

Ed & Debby

Thank you for allowing me to share a little of this incredibly painful and deeply personal time in my life. My hope is that you would be able to understand some of my grief, and in turn my great need for God to get through the agony of it—one minute at a time. God and His Word are the rock I clung to—then and now.

I have often mentioned the need to build strong relationships with God, our husbands, our families, and our friends. Never have I needed those relationships like I have in this deep sorrow. Ed was the only one who truly understood the depth of my pain, for we had lost our son together. We had walked side by side through many trials and tribulations during our marriage, but this was truly the worst of times. As we began the difficult steps of enduring the agony of grief, we were so blessed to have already learned how to lean on each other and to seek God together.

Ed was used to treating physical pain in his patients and compassionately caring for their emotional pain. But he was reminded again how much more difficult it is for our hearts to be healed. We needed to help each other keep our focus on the One who is our hope in the midst of despair. We needed to comfort one another as never before. Ecclesiastes 4:9-12 tells us, "Two are better than one, because they have a good return for their labor: If either of them falls down, one can help the other up. But pity anyone who falls and has no one to help them up. Also, if two lie down together, they will keep warm. But how can one keep warm alone? Though one may be overpowered, two can defend themselves. A cord of three strands is not quickly broken."

By ourselves, we can easily "snap" as a thin, single cord. We are sturdier when we are tightly bound to our husband, as two cords together. Strongest of all is to be woven as an indestructible cord of three strands—God, our husbands, and ourselves. We need to be entwined as a solid rope to withstand the struggles of this world and the lies of the Evil One.

In a time of tragedy, it is crucial to have the vital support that you will need. In the Scripture we just read in Ecclesiastes, Solomon revealed several advantages that come from healthy relationships. These include better profit, help in difficult times, comfort in times of need, and protection in times of danger. Ed and I certainly needed all of these. I am so thankful for all that God has taught Ed and me about building our relationship on His steadfast foundation. We would have crumbled without Him. We would have shattered and disconnected lives. We likely would have been overcome by despair without the love and prayers of His people holding us up. The burden of grief is eased by the knowledge that God is with us, that we are there for each other, and that we have dear family and friends to walk beside us on the difficult path of life.

My Side by Side group knew how much we needed support. They were an abundant source of comfort and strength for me during a time of great need. These dear women organized a twenty-four hour prayer vigil for the day of the funeral. Losing our precious son was the most difficult trial of my life. Laying Jon to rest was agonizing—for I buried a part of myself that day too.

These women knew how difficult that would be for us. They surrounded us with prayers, food, hugs, and love. They touched us deeply when we needed it most. Church friends, past and present, dropped everything to be with us, to comfort and encourage us. They laughed and cried with us as we celebrated Jon's life. We had shared our lives together, and I am so thankful that we had them to lift us up.

Our close relationships with our daughters, son-in-law, and sons have also made a huge difference as we have shared this painful journey. I am most thankful to God for my dear husband and for our "strong cord" as we walk through the valley of the shadow of death together.

Death has a way of putting life in perspective. It reminds us of what is truly important. It loudly proclaims how fleeting and fragile this life is. It compels us to freely forgive, to lavishly love, and to savor the gift of each day. It loudly proclaims our need for a right relationship with God and for His truths.

As I began to work on this book, I had no idea how mightily God would confirm the power of His Word. He could not have shown me in any more vivid way how very much I need Him and how very much I need the husband He has given me.

Favorite verses became even more meaningful, such as Moses' words to Joshua, "The LORD himself goes before you and will be with you; he will never leave you nor forsake you. Do not be afraid; do not be discouraged" (Deuteronomy 31:8). I claimed His promises while crying out to Him in my gut-wrenching grief with agonizing questions. *Why? Where were You? What if . . . ? How could a doctor and a nurse not "fix" an illness for their own child?*

God has remained steadfast in His comfort, faithful in His compassion, and bountiful in His love. Through a miracle of our life-giving God, the love my husband and I share brought Jon into this world. We named him Jonathan, meaning "God's gracious gift," which he truly was. Our love would sustain us now through our loss, as Jon left this world for the next. He is with our heavenly Father who embraces him now and also holds us tightly in His grasp and comforts us with the knowledge of the end of the story. One day we will all be together again in God's presence. What a promise! What a sweet reunion that will be!

Even as Ed and I hold hands and cry at the gravesite of our beloved son, we are held in the mighty hands of our Redeemer. We claim His Word that tells us, "Death has been swallowed up in victory. . . . Thanks be to God! He gives us the victory through our Lord Jesus Christ" (1 Corinthians 15:54,57).

Revelation 21:3-4 gives us a glimpse of heaven when God comes to dwell among us in the New Jerusalem, "And I heard a loud voice from the throne saying, 'Look! God's dwelling place is now among the people, and he will dwell with them. They will be his people, and God himself will be with them and be their God. He will wipe every tear from their eyes. There will be no more death or mourning or crying or pain, for the old order of things has passed away.'"

God's plans, purposes, and promises are trustworthy. On the one-year anniversary of Jon's death, our family gathered to laugh, cry, and pray together as we remembered Jon. The next day, we celebrated making it through that awful year by going out to dinner together. While we were at the restaurant, a huge thunderstorm came and went. As the sun came out again, we saw a magnificent rainbow appear in the sky. We felt God sent that perfect rainbow just for us, to remind us that He keeps His promises. Every single one of them.

Don't wait, dear one. Let God have your whole heart. Release your will to His eternal purposes. Let go of selfishness that never satisfies. Cling to His Word and His promises. Trust Him as you commit to do life His way. Build meaningful relationships where you share authentic life with one another.

Nurture a strong relationship with your husband. This is the life-partner God, in His infinite wisdom, gave you. He is a gift from the Lord to be appreciated, respected, and cherished. The reward will be great as you share the joys and sorrows of this life.

Fruitful in Suffering

What are you going through now that is causing you great pain and suffering? Is it a physical illness, a mentally taxing job, an emotionally stressful family situation, or a spiritually dry time? Jesus told His disciples in John 16:33, "I have told you these things, so that in me you may have peace. In this world you will have trouble. But take heart! I have overcome the world." Jesus is reminding us that we do have suffering and sorrow in this world. Yes, there are many rewards, joys, and celebrations as well. I thank God for those "mountaintop" times. However, have you ever noticed, that it is often in the "valley" times that we learn the most?

Remember the story of Elijah on Mount Carmel when he challenged the prophets of Baal? (1 Kings 18, 19) God mightily demonstrated His power when He sent fire to burn up the sacrifice, the wood, the stones, and even the water in the trench! The prophets of Baal clearly saw their god was a false god and there was only one true God.

Elijah, servant of the true God, witnessed this supernatural occurrence. Yet just a few verses later in Scripture, we find him afraid of Jezebel and running for his life! As we read of these events, we can clearly see how easy it is for us to go from the mountaintop high to the low valley of despair. What makes the difference? Could it be our focus? God is always God, but we can forget who He is, like Elijah did, when we take our eyes off of Him.

Focusing on truth makes a huge difference as it calms our fears, transforms our feelings, and shapes our thoughts. The Old Testament stories greatly encourage me in my walk with God. Reading about ordinary men and women who did the right thing are so helpful in pointing me to God.

Genesis tells of the fascinating life of Joseph, son of Jacob, who became the forefather of Israel. One bad thing after another happened to Joseph, from being sold into slavery by his jealous brothers to being falsely accused of attempted sexual assault by Potiphar's wife and imprisoned. Remarkably, even while in prison Joseph kept his focus on God. He allowed God to use that difficult time to prepare him for the future. God was with Joseph, freed him from prison, and blessed his life.

In her book, *Laying My Isaac Down,* which was inspired by a painful life experience, Carol Kent shares an insight about being fruitful in our suffering. The naming of Joseph's two sons tells of his steadfast heart. "Joseph named his firstborn Manasseh and said, 'It is because God has made me forget all my trouble and all my father's household.' The second son he named Ephraim and said, 'It is because God has made me fruitful in the land of my suffering,'" (Genesis 41:51-52). Later in Joseph's story, we find that he is second in command to Pharaoh, in a position to save his family during the famine. He was indeed fruitful in the Lord's purposes for him. I desire to be fruitful in my suffering. Don't you?

With sincere honesty I can say that I have learned much more about God in my suffering—especially in the suffering of grief—than I have learned any other way. When life is hard, I have gained greater knowledge of who He is—and who I am in Him. We learn this as we depend on Him and allow Him to use these life experiences for His glory.

In *Touched by His Unseen Hand,* Jennifer Rothschild says it well, "It captivates us to see someone confined and constrained by trials and calamity still bear the fruit of peace and righteousness. That's when God's glory is truly seen, because it can only be God fashioning such beauty from the elements of certain despair." She reminds us that "Sometimes, God allows hard things to come into our lives to refine us and form us into a vessel that radiates His glory."

We truly want God to make us into vessels refined for His use and His glory. Don't we? However, we sure don't want to face the hard things of life. Unfortunately, they are unavoidable. Scripture makes it clear that life is full of hardships. Lamentations, the only book of the Bible consisting solely of laments, is a testament of this. How reassuring to read these words, "Because of the Lord's great love, we are not consumed, for his compassions never fail. They are new every morning; great is your faithfulness" (Lamentations 3:22-23).

God is big enough to handle our tough questions. He loves us enough to be patient and compassionate as we pour out the intense emotions of our struggling hearts. He was there when Kayla, a resident's wife, asked, "God, why does it seem like everyone around me is fertile while I have been trying for four years to have a child with no success? Why are you not blessing us? Why is it taking so long? Will you ever give us a child?" It was difficult for Kayla to sit through some of our Bible study discussions that were focused, at times, on children. She sat hurting in silence.

Then one evening, Kayla happily accepted my invitation and joined me for dinner before one of our meetings. As she shared her pain, I was drawn to her heartache and felt the need to pray for her.

She was able to open up to the other women later that night about her longing and they began to pray for her, too. God taught her so much in those years of waiting. She learned to depend on Him and her relationship with her husband grew deeper and stronger. She also realized her hope was not to be in a good job or in the blessing of a child. Her hope was to be found in God alone.

What a thrill it was when God blessed Kayla and her husband with a beautiful healthy boy. Their joy was multiplied even further when she found out that she was expecting again. Praise God for His goodness and His perfect timing. Thank God that He is with us in the waiting and that His answer is always right—even if He chooses to bless us in a way we don't expect.

The Paradox of Pain

One of the primary ways God can use suffering in our lives is when we show His compassion to those who are suffering around us. "Praise be to the God and Father of our Lord Jesus Christ, the Father of compassion and the God of all comfort, who comforts us in all our troubles, so that we can comfort those in any trouble with the comfort we ourselves receive from God" (2 Corinthians 1:3-4). He comforts us, and then we pass it on!

Early on in the grieving process, I learned that it was very easy for me to become too self-focused. People knew I was hurting and didn't want to "bother" me by sharing their own struggles—which to them seemed small by comparison. Surprisingly, I found it helpful to take my eyes off myself and encourage people that I wanted to know of their sorrow, too. I found healing for my own pain in ministering to the hurts of others, in caring about them, in comforting them, and in praying for them. It is a holy paradox—the Holy Spirit works through us to comfort others and then, miraculously, we find the comfort we crave.

Ordinary as I am, I have experienced God holding my hand and carrying my heart through this painful experience. He has better equipped me for His extraordinary purposes. He has used the Refiner's fire to make my life better reflect Him. Through faith, I am "shielded by God's power until the coming of the salvation that is ready to be revealed in the last time. In all this you greatly rejoice, though now for a little while you may have had to suffer grief in all kinds of trials. These have come so that the proven genuineness of your faith—of greater worth than gold, which perishes even though refined by fire—may result in praise, glory and honor when Jesus Christ is revealed" (1 Peter 1:5-7).

Suffering is one thing we all have in common. People are all around us who are going through trials. Not long ago, I was at the gym, sitting on the bench in order to put my shoes on, when a woman next to me who I had never spoken to before finished a conversation with a friend and then turned to me. I said, "It sounds like you are having a difficult time, I am so sorry." Amy then shared with me about her husband who was having a change in mental status causing him to spend money unwisely and "yell" at her much of the time. She seemed deeply touched by my offer to pray for her, and I did—right there in the gym. Why? Because God had comforted me, opened my eyes to the pain of others, and had equipped me to comfort her, too.

Another example occurred two days later when I went for a dental appointment. While scheduling my next cleaning, I asked the receptionist if she had any fun plans for the weekend. She explained that she was going to a conference and was nervous about the trip. I offered, "I will pray for you." Her eyes began to overflow with tears, and she then told me that she had a "suspicious" mammogram the day before and they thought she had cancer. As I listened, I felt such compassion for her that I found myself fighting back tears too. She stood up, took my hand, and said, "Thank you for praying. I need it. I have not shared this with any of the office staff." I barely know her, but I am praying for her because I care about what she is going through.

A recent e-mail from a dear friend saddened me deeply. Her teenage son is struggling with depression and dark thoughts. He ran away and they didn't know where he was for several days. Another friend, who is the wife of a physician, has had a difficult year with frequent migraines. This amazing wife and mother of four children has been incapacitated much of the time due to these headaches. Her attitude has been inspiring as she has kept her focus on God while persevering through the pain. It is difficult, too, for her husband who is busy with his practice and unable to help as much as he would like to.

Offering to help with the children, cleaning, or preparing meals in such a difficult situation is not my response because I am such a good person. It is only because I serve such a good God. He lovingly comforts me with His compassion in ways that minister deep in my soul. I can't help but let some of it overflow to the hurting people around me. These examples and many others happened in my life over the course of just one week. Not by coincidence, but by divine design. How about your connections? Who around you needs His consolation to ease their pain?

The Path to Freedom

Many times, I don't understand God's ways. I can't figure out the seeming inconsistency of stories like Peter being miraculously escorted out of prison by an angel (Acts 12:1-18), while John the

Baptist was beheaded in prison (Matthew 14:3-12). God could have rescued John as well. God certainly was able to change the outcome for my Jon. But through His Word, God reminds me, "As the heavens are higher than the earth, so are my ways higher than your ways and my thoughts than your thoughts" (Isaiah 55:9). This is where faith— "confidence in what we hope for and assurance about what we do not see" (Hebrews 11:1)—and trust become our anchor.

Affliction, suffering, hardship, disease, dashed dreams, disappointment, and death—the list goes on and on. Jesus was "despised and rejected by mankind, a man of suffering, and familiar with pain. Like one from whom people hide their faces he was despised, and we held him in low esteem" (Isaiah 53:3). He understands our sorrows, our struggles, our pain.

As always, Jesus gives us the example we need to follow in our suffering. In the Garden of Gethsemane, He was facing agony that I cannot begin to imagine. Jesus was preparing to take every sin ever committed—past, present, and future—upon Himself for us. Jesus told his disciples, "'My soul is overwhelmed with sorrow to the point of death. Stay here and keep watch with me.' Going a little farther, he fell with his face to the ground and prayed, 'My Father, if it is possible, may this cup be taken from me. Yet not as I will, but as you will,'" (Matthew 26:38-39).

Jesus knew the burden of the sin He would bear. Think about the enormity of the sins you know about and then imagine those of all people, for all time. No wonder Luke, the astute physician, records that when Jesus prayed in His anguish, "his sweat was like drops of blood falling to the ground" (Luke 22:44). Knowing what He was facing, Jesus wanted the cup of suffering taken from Him. But even more, He wanted to submit to the Father, so He willingly obeyed—despite the incredible cost.

This is our example, suffering with our focus on the Father's will. What are you suffering with today that you need to submit to God and then trust Him to use for today and for many tomorrows? In the midst of my pain, my heart joyfully cries out, "Thank you, Jesus, for your obedience even unto death. Thank you, Jesus, that Your sacrifice makes it possible for me—and all of us—to spend eternity with You."

Nancy Guthrie, who bears the pain of losing two infant children, writes in her book, *The One Year Book of Hope,* "While Jesus tells us not to run from suffering, He suggests we do more than simply endure it. He admonishes us to embrace it. He wants us to stop feeling sorry for ourselves and to focus on what there is to learn in the suffering. He invites us to draw closer to him in the midst of our suffering. There's freedom there, and he is inviting us into the glory and joy of it.

"To embrace suffering is to welcome God's work in your life even in the most unimaginable circumstances. To embrace suffering is to enjoy God's presence in your life even when you are filled with questions for him. To embrace suffering is to enter into a deeper relationship with God that you could not have enjoyed without experiencing penetrating pain. The suffering not only makes you crave such a relationship, it gives you the capacity to savor it. Ultimately, to embrace suffering is to allow your now broken heart to be more easily broken by the things that break the heart of God. To embrace suffering is to become more aware of and more apt to engage with the suffering of the world around you. Don't run from suffering; embrace it and you will find yourself enriched and renewed."

I'm not there yet. I can't completely embrace the agonizing grief at this time. But I do want to and God is showing me how, one step at a time as He holds my hand. I am a tottering toddler now, but one day I shall run freely. Will you run with me? Will you allow God to use your vulnerability in hardships as a safe place for others to share their burdens and as an instrument to point them to God? Sadly, we don't often find people who will openly share their struggles in our churches or our neighborhoods. Be a beacon—a breath of refreshing air.

Jesus can calm the storms in our lives. He is the very One who rebuked the wind and the waves, thereby calming the storm the disciples were fearful of. What raging storm are you fearful of? "Do not fear, for I have redeemed you; I have summoned you by name; you are mine. When you pass through the waters, I will be with you; and when you pass through the rivers, they will not sweep over you. When you walk through the fire, you will not be burned; the flames will not set you ablaze" (Isaiah 43:1-2).

I want God's will for my life—no matter the cost. The expense is great, but Jesus has already paid the price. Moses' words from God in Deuteronomy 30:19-20 powerfully challenge me: "that you may love the Lord your God, listen to his voice, and hold fast to him."

My dear friend, "when troubles come your way, consider it an opportunity for great joy. For you know that when your faith is tested, your endurance has a chance to grow. So, let it grow, for when your endurance is fully developed, you will be perfect and complete needing nothing" (James 1:2-4 NLT). Let's respond to the suffering of this world with strong faith. Hold fast to Him! Choose life—choose the Lord.

Rx: Embrace suffering one day at a time, while focusing on your future in eternity.

Chapter 10

℞ Healing for the Heart

Name : _____   Age : _____

Address : _____   Date : _____

Who can discern his errors? Forgive my hidden faults.

—Psalm 19:12

Label ☐

Refill 0 1 2 3 4 5 PRN

H as there been a time in your life when you needed surgery? If so, you probably checked out the reputation of the surgeon. Perhaps your husband knew them professionally. Maybe you were referred by a trusted friend. But regardless of the connection, you needed to be sure that you could trust this doctor and that you would be in "good hands" before you consented to the operation.

We can rest easily that we are indeed in "Good Hands"—the trustworthy, competent, and righteous hands of our heavenly Father. As we have studied Psalm 19, we have learned that the truth of God's law revives us, makes us wise, gives joy to our heart, gives light to our eyes, warns us, and rewards us. But there is a turn in reflection in verse 12, as the psalmist begins to look inward. What a sharp contrast we see between man's sinfulness and finiteness in light of God's perfection, infinite glory, power, and wisdom displayed in His magnificent creation and mighty Word.

This verse asks us, "Who can discern his errors?" Here we find ourselves laid bare before the God who sees all. *Nothing* is hidden from Him. As a result, the godly woman stands in fear of hidden faults that may be unknown to her. The sinful woman trembles, as she knows her errors well.

It is time that we allow the Great Physician to examine our hearts—and every aspect of our lives. Just as we experience trepidation when we are about to undergo surgery on our natural bodies, we are fearful of allowing God to use His exploratory surgical instruments to closely examine our hearts. This is when we truly see who we are in relation to who He is—there is no place to hide from His truth.

Scripture explains in Hebrews 4:12, "For the word of God is alive and active. Sharper than any double-edged sword, it penetrates even to dividing soul and spirit, joints and marrow; it judges the thoughts and attitudes of the heart." What a powerful description of the Word of God. It is as sharp as the surgeon's scalpel as it carefully dissects through every layer. We have already learned that we can trust this Great Surgeon. Let's allow Him to skillfully use His mighty scalpel to excise the disease in our hearts and return us to good spiritual health.

The process of physical surgery is painful, often followed by a long and difficult recovery. Yet, we voluntarily choose to endure this suffering for the potential benefits it will bring. Let's willingly enter God's "operating room," trusting Him to bring about miraculous healing that only He can, knowing we will receive tender, loving care from this compassionate Physician.

The humble woman's response to heart surgery is to ask God to "forgive my hidden faults." She desires true godliness. The arrogant woman has no regard for God and continues in her sin, not allowing God to heal her heart. Lord, help us to be humble and contrite of heart as we come to You for the cure we need.

Removing a Root of Bitterness

If you are like me, you have found yourself in need of spiritual "heart surgery" many times. It is a piercing, disquieting ordeal to endure, followed by a challenging time of mending. But, it is well worth the discomfort for the refreshing and new health it brings.

Many years ago, as a new believer, I read Colossians 3:13, "Bear with each other and forgive one another if any of you has a grievance against someone. Forgive as the Lord forgave you." God immediately pricked my heart with His scalpel. It was as though I saw my sin of unforgiveness for the first time. As God placed me under His examination light, a root of bitterness was clearly seen spreading throughout my body, devouring vital organs in its path.

At the time, we had just moved to a new state where Ed began his residency, and we were blessed with our first child a month later. I had harbored much anger against my parents for the issues that had occurred in my dysfunctional childhood home, but I didn't realize how much this had affected me until I was led by God to examine my thoughts. I found myself thinking things like, *This is their first grandchild. I will get even with them by making sure they never get to see this child. Then they can't hurt her like they have hurt me.* Yes, ugly thoughts to be sure, but I hadn't really considered how "stinking" my thinking was. The evils of parental alcohol abuse had colored my world in ways I was unaware of.

Wanting to be obedient in my new walk with the Lord, I took my first big step of faith and asked God to forgive me and help me to forgive my parents. I felt it was necessary to go to them in person to ask for their forgiveness. In my mind, the things I had done "wrong" were minor compared to the sins of my mom and dad, but God continued to nudge me. I knew that in His eyes I too had sinned and needed to make things right.

So I asked Ed if Kristi and I could travel the 600 miles to their home. Many hurdles stood in the way, as I knew Ed did not have the time to go with me and we really couldn't afford for me to fly.

But as medical wives, we must learn to do a lot of things independently, and I needed to get used to this way of life and be able to travel by myself. Despite the expense, Ed and I agreed that the trip was important enough for me to proceed with plans to fly there.

With some apprehension, I made my preparations to travel. I had been praying and asked many others to pray with me. This would be the first time my parents would meet Kristi, their first grandchild, but they were shocked that I would come alone with her. On the second day of the visit, I told them my main reason for coming was to ask for their forgiveness. I explained everything that God had shown me through His Word and how I wanted to reconcile our relationship. The talk did not go as I had expected. They were angry and accused me of trying to "dredge up the past." I was profoundly disappointed in their reaction and many tears followed.

But despite my disappointment, at the same time I experienced a supernatural change in myself that I can only describe as the feeling of a huge weight being lifted from my shoulders. I felt an amazing peace. I did not realize until then that I was not harming them by not forgiving. I was hurting myself and all of my relationships—with God and others. God impressed on my heart that I had done what I needed to do. It was harder than I had imagined, but the change inside of me was remarkably, positively freeing.

I know now that God used that time to change my mom and dad, too. It took eighteen more years to see the fruit, but the seeds were planted then. They both became believers before their deaths. God allowed me the privilege of praying with them to receive Christ as they each faced death from cancer. We had joyful years together with a reconciled relationship, and I am so grateful for that gift of time in a right relationship with them. Praise God for His marvelous

Word that pierces and transforms me to better reflect Him. I shudder to think what my life would have been like if I had continued to hang on to that unforgiving spirit.

Since then, there have been many times when I have been tempted to stay angry and try to intentionally hurt someone by not forgiving them. But I know now that it hurts me so much more and really hinders my walk with God. I remember how He has forgiven me. As I recall what He miraculously does through forgiveness, I am motivated to once again forgive.

A friend of mine is struggling to forgive her ex-husband. She often speaks of him in negative words and feels that it is just too hard to forgive him. My heart breaks for her as I see how this bitterness toward him is causing her physical and spiritual illness. I pray for her to be able to take this excruciating, but necessary, step to choose to forgive and forget, not because he deserves it, but because God loves her and has given her the example to follow in Christ's death on the cross. The cross was more than enough to pay for every sin. My sins. Your sins. Our husbands' sins.

We all have times in life when forgiveness is needed. "Wrongs" are either done against us or we commit an offense against someone else. Either way, we can and should make the first move to restore the relationship. Ephesians 4:31-32 reminds us to, "Get rid of all bitterness, rage and anger, brawling and slander, along with every form of malice. Be kind and compassionate to one another, forgiving each other, just as in Christ God forgave you."

Focusing on God's forgiveness in our lives motivates us to forgive others. That release means letting them "off the hook" and showing them the same exact mercy God has shown us. Mark Twain says it well when he wrote, "Forgiveness is the fragrance the violet sheds on the heel that crushed it."

Forgiveness doesn't mean that there are not consequences for wrong actions. It also does not mean we will always totally forget what has happened. *Webster's* defines *forget* as "to lose the remembrance of; be unable to think of or recall; to treat with inattention or disregard; to disregard intentionally: overlook; to cease remembering or noticing." We are human. Only God is supernaturally able to forgive *and* forget, as He tells us in Isaiah 43:25, ". . . I am he who blots out your transgressions, for my own sake, and remembers your sins no more." But with the help of God's mighty power working in us, we can choose to disregard hurtful things and allow forgiveness to start the healing process in our hearts.

Conquering Anger

It can be hard to overlook offenses committed against us. These transgressions occur in different ways, but often the culprit comes in the form of harsh words spoken to us that hurt our feelings and stir up more ugliness in our hearts. Scripture has a lot to say about anger. In one biblical search, 270 verses were listed as having the word "anger" in them. Many of these refer to God's anger toward sin. This is a righteous anger. This is very different from the irritation displayed in us as sinful men and women.

Our embittered responses are usually self-focused, such as when we don't get our way or our ego is bruised. In the practical writings of James, we find this advice, "My dear brothers and sisters, take note of this: Everyone should be quick to listen, slow to speak and slow to become angry, because human anger does not produce the righteousness that God desires" (James 1:19-20). This is so to the point—as God knows well our tendency to not listen to others, to talk for the sake of self being heard, and to quickly become angry.

Proverbs 15:1, a verse with which I am very familiar, states, "A gentle answer turns away wrath, but a harsh word stirs up anger." I know that when I hear a harsh word, especially from my husband, it does indeed stir up anger! If I am aware of this, then why do I respond in a bad temper instead of giving a gentle response? I have the choice to either add fuel to the fire of the heated moment or quench the fire with gentle words. Oh, what a slow learner I am to do things God's way! I do not accomplish my desire to live a righteous life when I give in to my sinful nature instead of honoring God.

My friend Jennifer, also married to a physician, related a story to me about an argument she and her husband had on the way to church. *Church?* Yes, most of us can relate. We are on our way to worship God and our minds and hearts want to be focused on Him. Yet, bitter words often come out of our mouths as we travel to His house! Clearly, Satan does not want us arriving with the right heart attitude. He knows that hard feelings cause us to lose our ability to concentrate on the Lord and worship Him in spirit and in truth.

This particular day was one of those times for Jennifer and her husband. She wanted to be on time to teach Sunday School and needed to leave by 9:30 in order to be there before 10:00. At 9:30 they were in the car, when her husband mentioned that he planned to make a quick stop at Starbucks on the way because he didn't have enough time to get his second cup of coffee at home.

Jennifer impatiently replied, "We do not have time to stop. You should have planned ahead for your coffee fix. After all, I made enough for you to have two cups at home. You knew I needed to be on time, as I told you last night."

He harshly responded, "It will only take a few minutes, and we do have time. I am stopping." This disagreement continued back and forth all the way to the church parking lot. Neither one of them had "warm feelings" toward one another or a right heart attitude as they entered the building. Then, during the service, he was unexpectedly called to come to the hospital, leaving Jennifer to find another ride home. Worse than that, they never really had time to talk about what happened. They were both left with tension in the relationship. This pattern seemed to repeat often and they were both growing very weary of the constant strife.

Jennifer and I discussed several practical ideas, concluding that she needed to work smarter, not harder. She was already working hard on their relationship. She needed to channel her effort and energy into making wiser and more beneficial choices, discerning what would build up and not tear down their marriage.

At one point during our discussion, Jennifer posed this very common question, "Which one of us was right?" How easy it is to think, more often than not, that there is a wrong person and a right person. Of course, we usually see ourselves as the "right" one.

She was thinking something like, *He is so inconsiderate. I did tell him I needed to be on time. He doesn't seem to care about me. All he can think about is himself and his need for coffee. To add to that, he acts so unloving with his harsh tone.*

He was thinking more along the lines of, *Gee whiz, it's only a few minutes, why does she get so uptight? She can be so controlling at times. We had plenty of time. Why does she have to use that disrespectful attitude with me and treat me like one of the kids?*

It is so much easier to look from the outside in and see that neither one of them was right. They were both being selfish and concerned about their desires only. Jennifer and I talked about how to respond in a way that honored God and her husband. We agreed that gently and lovingly saying words such as, "I am concerned that I might be late, and I really do want to be on time to teach. At the same time, you are more important to me than time and I am willing to stop if you really feel you need to."

In this way, she is communicating honestly about her desire to be on time, but she is also letting him know that what he wants is important to her. She is choosing to be respectful and other-centered. Yes, this is so hard to do, yet so much better for both of them. He could honor her request to be on time and forego his desire for coffee. Or, perhaps, lovingly express his need to stop. In other words, he could also choose to be other-centered.

Arguments occur many times when we simply want our own way. Scripture confronts this reality when it asks, "What causes fights and quarrels among you? Don't they come from your desires that battle within you?" (James 4:1). When two people have the same self-centered desires, the result is ugly and destructive to the relationship.

As women, we struggle with some really difficult scenarios. One doctor's wife asked, "How do I deal with the fact that he seems to have plenty of energy to do what he needs to do at work, but seems to have no energy to invest in the work of relationships when he is home? This makes me angry, and I am not sure how to handle these intense feelings."

Ephesians 4:26-27 advises, "'In your anger do not sin': Do not let the sun go down while you are still angry, and do not give the devil a foothold." Three wise challenges are given. First, we can't help but feel anger at times—it is a human emotion given to us by God. He reminds us, however, not to sin in that anger. Express your anger to God. Then allow His Holy Spirit to lead you and His Word to guide you to react in a godly way. We can honestly express how we feel in a kind way without giving full vent to our anger. This builds relationships instead of tearing them down.

Secondly, we need to deal with our anger as soon as possible. Just as a closed boil can fester and become infected if left untreated, our hearts can become infected with sin if we dwell on our hurt and allow the anger to grow. It is best to deal with the issue quickly while it is still today. For many of us, that may require writing down our thoughts in a note or an e-mail to communicate with our husbands who may be unavailable to talk with that day. Or it may mean setting up a time in the near future when you can talk.

Lastly, we are reminded to "not give the devil a foothold." We are not to allow Satan any opportunity to wreak havoc in our relationships. Beware of his subtle tricks—they are so easy to overlook.

Your Real Enemy

When we moved to Virginia, I was thrilled to have a milder climate to be able to do more gardening. I soon became aware of other creatures that like the warmth too. I discovered they made puzzling patterns on the surface of my yard as they tunneled underground. To my dismay, there were also bushes dying due to their roots being eaten. I pulled one up one day to discover it had no roots at all. A friend explained that moles like to dig underground to find their favorite meal of grubs. Apparently the voles later follow behind in these tunnels (after the moles do all the work) to find their favorite food—roots. Hmmm. They are not easy to purge once you have them.

Scripture tells us in 1 Peter 5:8 that our "enemy the devil prowls around like a roaring lion looking for someone to devour." Many times we are unaware of the damage he is doing because he works in subtle ways below the surface, just like the "vole" he is. He takes advantage of our unresolved hard feelings, much like those unattended mole's tunnels. He burrows deep—quietly and secretly with his devastating destruction.

One of Satan's highest priorities is to destroy—or at least hinder—a marriage. Your marriage reflects God's love and Christ's sacrifice (Ephesians 5:25) to those around you. Satan does not want this witness so he tries to convince us that our spouse is our enemy. But I want to remind you—your husband is not the enemy. This is worth repeating even though we have mentioned it before. It may feel like he is your adversary when you are having an argument or are dealing with some consequence of his demanding schedule, but your husband is not your foe. Satan is the enemy! We must make ourselves alert to his schemes.

"Submit yourselves, then, to God. Resist the devil and he will flee from you." These wise words in James 4:7 remind us that the Enemy flees when confronted with the life, death, and resurrection of Jesus Christ. God has already won the war with Satan (Revelation 12:10-12). We simply need to rebuke him with the fact that he has already lost the battle that Jesus' sacrifice won for us. He knows his dark deeds cannot prevail when exposed to the brilliant light of Jesus.

We are directed in Ephesians 6:10-11 to "be strong in the Lord and in his mighty power. Put on the full armor of God so that you can take your stand against the devil's schemes." To battle our Enemy, we must know his tactics. To stand against him, we must have all of our protective gear on and our weapons ready. To disarm him, we must recognize his methods and respond with godly warfare.

One common trap of the Enemy that I too often fall into is focusing only on the offenses of others, while not considering my own transgressions. Matthew 7:5 reminds me, "You hypocrite, first take the plank out of your own eye, and then you will see clearly to remove the speck from your brother's eye." This approach would surely help us in many marital issues, wouldn't it?

Recently, I had a conflict with my husband over stirring peanut butter. Yes, I am ashamed to admit to this truth—especially over such a silly topic. Unfortunately, I have found that it is usually the small things and not the big ones that often cause arguments. But on that particular morning, I was stirring a new jar of the natural peanut butter—the kind where the oil tends to separate from the peanut paste. When my thoughtful husband entered the kitchen and saw me struggling to properly stir the mixture, he offered to take over. I appreciated his kindness and gladly accepted his offer.

When I came back into the kitchen a while later to spread peanut butter on my banana bread, I took one look at the contents and without thinking, blurted out, "This jar is not stirred!" Of course, what I meant was that it was not stirred enough to satisfy my expectations. With one look at Ed, I knew that I had offended him. His response confirmed my impression. The more I tried to explain my perspective, the more hurt he looked. I should have kept my mouth shut. I could either have eaten it as it was or could have chosen to stir it more myself. But I felt he had overreacted—which was ironic, since that term usually describes me—and that the issue was with him.

Soon, I felt that familiar small voice of the Lord prompting me. "Humble yourself and make the first move to restore this relationship." As I apologized to Ed, he graciously forgave me. Later on we could even laugh about how ridiculous it was to argue over something so insignificant.

Notice that in this situation, God spoke to me through the principles and truth of His Word. He did it in a way that convicted me of my sin and motivated me to do the right actions or say the right words for the right reasons. It is almost as though God woos me back to a righteous relationship with Him and with others around me. Listening to Him and following through leads to harmony and peace and joy in my soul.

Condemnation vs. Conviction

Satan uses another tactic on us that is quite subtle and deceptive. A master of condemnation and accusation, first he tells us that the problem is the other person's fault and not our own. Then he tells us that we are a bad person for arguing with others, for losing our temper, for saying the nasty things we have said. He whispers that we are a bad wife, a bad mother, a bad friend. Then his goal is accomplished, for we feel overwhelmed by guilt, somehow thinking we should be—as though we must pay for the sins ourselves.

Now is the time to remind the Enemy of this priceless fact: Jesus has already paid the full price for our sins! It has taken me a long time to realize that God's voice does not bring guilt—it leads me to repentance and restoration. Satan's accusations lead to condemnation and cripple my ability to go forward in taking healthy steps to resolve the issues. But the Holy Spirit *convicts* me in order to show me my sin and lead me to change my behavior.

Scripture sheds light on the disparity between conviction and condemnation as we look at the life of Peter contrasted with the life of Judas. In Matthew 26:69-75 we are told of Peter's denial (three times) of knowing Jesus. His guilt and shame must have been immense as "Peter remembered the word Jesus had spoken . . . he went outside and wept bitterly."

Later, we learn that after His resurrection, Jesus talked to Peter on the beach (John 21:15-17). Jesus asks Peter three times—no coincidence—if he loved Him. Peter answered yes each time and Jesus told him to "take care of my sheep." Jesus wanted to know if Peter was really willing to commit his life to serving God. Peter understood that he had been forgiven by the One who makes forgiveness possible. He was being given a commission to tell others about Jesus. In that moment, Peter truly became a man who would serve God wholeheartedly the rest of his life.

The story of Judas was tragically different. "When Judas, who had betrayed him, saw that Jesus was condemned, he was seized with remorse and returned the thirty silver coins to the chief priests and the elders. 'I have sinned,' he said, 'for I have betrayed innocent blood.' 'What is that to us?' they replied. 'That's your responsibility.' So Judas threw the money into the temple and left. Then he went away and hanged himself" (Matthew 27:3-5).

Judas had betrayed Jesus like Peter. But the difference in outcome hinged on their responses. The conviction of the Holy Spirit led Peter to repent, as he sought and received Jesus' forgiveness. Judas' overwhelming guilt led to his demise.

We must know God's Word in order to be prepared for the spiritual battles that lie ahead. 1 John 1:9 assures us, "If we confess our sins, he is faithful and just and will forgive us our sins and purify us from all unrighteousness." The truth is that He forgives us when we ask Him to. Completely. Forever. Praise Him for this gift of perfect forgiveness that is ours simply for the asking.

The Gift of Reconciliation

Some time ago Ed and I recalled with sadness how his fellow residents were doing, five years after residency. Half of them were divorced. We knew many of them well enough to know that a lack of forgiveness was a primary cause in the downfall of their marriages.

The words of Charlotte Bronte aptly apply here, "Life appears to me to be too short to be spent in nursing hurts or registering wrongs." Pointing fingers, on top of the stresses already present in a resident's marriage, did not help matters.

Our good friends, Leslie and Mitch, were among the casualties. She resented how much time he was spending at the hospital and berated him for it. He felt she was an inadequate wife and mother and told her so in many ways. He had an affair. He did not repent.

Reconciliation was needed so badly, but Leslie simply could not forgive. We loved them and tried desperately to help them rebuild their broken relationship, but to no avail. Certainly, it was a seemingly impossible relationship to reconcile. But our great God of redemption and miracles specializes in the impossible. Unfortunately, they simply never gave Him a chance to restore their home.

Walter Wangerin Jr. shares these words in *As for Me and My House:*

Forgiveness is a willing relinquishment of certain rights. The one sinned against chooses not to demand her rights of redress for the hurt she has suffered. She does not hold her spouse accountable for his sin, nor enforce a punishment upon him, nor exact a payment from him as in "reparations." She does not make his life miserable in order to balance accounts for her own misery, though she might feel perfectly justified in doing so, tit for tat: "He deserves to be hurt as he has hurt me." In this way (please note this carefully) she steps outside the systems of the law; she steps into the world of mercy. She makes possible a whole new economy for their relationship: not the cold-blooded and killing machinery of rules, rights and privileges, but the tender and nourishing care of mercy, which always rejoices in the growth, not the guilt or the pain of the other. This is sacrifice. To give up one's rights is to sacrifice something of one's self—something hard fought for in the world.

Sometimes we need help from a counselor, or a pastor, or wise advice from a trusted friend to aid us in discerning what God wants us to do to get back on the right track with our relationships. An excellent resource for resolving personal conflict biblically is *The Peacemaker* by Ken Sande. We found it to be insightful and very helpful for personal, family, and church relationships, as Ed and I participated in a seminar based on this book at a former church where he served as an elder.

Sande reminds us of Romans 12:21, "Do not be overcome by evil, but overcome evil with good," when he says:

> Most people will respond favorably to the peace-making principles set forth in Scripture. At times, however, you may encounter someone who simply refuses to be reconciled with you. As a result of bitterness, pride, mistrust, or greed, some people will persistently ignore repentance, reject confrontation, and resist co-operative negotiation. Sometimes a person will even continue to purposely mistreat you. The natural reaction is to strike back or at least stop doing anything good to that person. Jesus commands us to take a re-markably different course of action when we encounter such treatment: "But I tell you who hear me: Love your

enemies, do good to those who hate you, bless those
who curse you, pray for those who mistreat you. . . .
Then your reward will be great, and you will be the
sons of the Most High, because he is kind to the un-
grateful and wicked. Be merciful, just as your Father is
merciful" (Luke 6:27-28, 35-36).

I find great comfort in knowing that God called David a man
after his own heart, despite David's sins. After his sin of adultery
with Bathsheba and the subsequent murder of her husband, David
came to God in repentance when he cried out, "Create in me a pure
heart, O God, and renew a steadfast spirit within me" (Psalm 51:10).
This was some serious sin, and David knew it. He was physically
wasting away due to his guilt. He knew his only hope was to have
his holy God cleanse him and give him a pure heart.

God brings us back to Himself when He forgives our sins and
makes us righteous again. Once we are reconciled to God, we have
the privilege and responsibility to encourage others to do likewise.
Second Corinthians 5:18-21 explains, "All this is from God, who reconciled us to himself through Christ and gave us the ministry of reconciliation: that God was reconciling the world to himself in Christ,
not counting men's sins against them. And he has committed to us
the message of reconciliation. We are therefore Christ's ambassadors,
as though God were making his appeal through us. We implore you
on Christ's behalf: Be reconciled to God. God made him who had no
sin to be sin for us, so that in him we might become the righteousness
of God."

These wonderful words tell us that we are God's official ambassadors to the world for the restoration of relationships. Let's begin
with the relationships in our own lives that need to be mended. Let's

encourage each other to do the hard work that brings healing. Then let's spread this healing balm all over this world.

Serving Out Of Love

When God touches us in the deepest recesses of our hearts with His amazing forgiveness—freely given in love—we can't help but want to extend that forgiveness to others. Conversely, our lack of forgiveness may come from not truly understanding what we have been forgiven.

A favorite book of mine is *The Prodigal God* by Timothy Keller. He does a phenomenal job of really digging into the familiar parable of the prodigal son, found in Luke 15. Keller gives deep insight into the heart of the father in the story, who represents Father God. He explains that both brothers are alienated from God and seek a different way into the kingdom of heaven. We can easily see how lost the younger brother is with the choices he makes. Thankfully, this son does eventually receive the grace the father is freely giving when he is graciously welcomed home and his return is lavishly celebrated.

When we look closely, however, we see the older brother is separated from the father by his own self-righteousness. He doesn't even realize how lost he is. He is prideful of what he has done "right" and doesn't see where his heart is wrong. Keller writes, "Elder brothers don't go to God and beg for healing from their condition. They see nothing wrong with their condition, and that can be fatal. If you know you are sick, you may go to a doctor; if you don't know you're sick you won't—you'll just die."

We must recognize our need for Jesus in order to truly understand what he has done for us. He saved us at an incredible cost to Himself. Compared to the price He paid, the cost of following Him is minuscule. He initiates the love. We only need to respond by repenting and recognizing our need for Him.

When we truly grasp God's great love and His sacrifice for the forgiveness of our sins, we want to respond by forgiving others. We want to become more like Him. We want to love the Father in a much deeper way and serve Him wholeheartedly in return. How do we serve Him with pure motives and pure hearts? I'm not sure I have the best answer to this, but I do know it begins with asking Christ into our hearts and then allowing Him to take over everything.

Robert Boyd Munger, in a beloved piece of literature entitled *My Heart—Christ's Home,* uses Paul's words in Ephesians 3:16-17, "That [God] may grant you to be strengthened with might through his Spirit in the inner man, and that Christ may dwell in your hearts through faith." Such awesome truth that Christ Himself, through the Holy Spirit, can enter a heart and be at home there—at least as much as we will let Him "settle in."

Munger paints a revealing word picture as he walks us through nine "rooms" of our heart. The opportunity is provided for us to examine our lives one aspect at a time. For example, Jesus tells the man in the story that there is a bad odor coming from the hall closet. The man does not want to deal with the bad things in his life that he is hiding from Jesus. Reluctantly, he hands Jesus the key to the closet and says sadly, "'But you have to open the closet and clean it out. I haven't the strength to do it.' 'I know,' he said. 'I know you haven't. Just give me the key. Just authorize me to handle that closet and I will.'

"So, with trembling fingers, I passed the key over to him. He took it from my hand, walked over to the door, opened it, entered it, took out the putrefying stuff that was rotting there, and threw it all away. Then he cleansed the closet, painted it, and fixed it up all in a moment's time. Immediately, a fresh, fragrant breeze swept through the house. The whole atmosphere changed. What release and victory to have that dead thing out of my life! No matter what sin or pain might be in my past, Jesus is ready to forgive, to heal, and to make me whole."

You may be thinking, *This really makes sense. I do believe that Scripture has the better way to do life, and I do desire to handle conflict in a godly way. But it is so hard.* Even as I write this chapter, I find myself thinking back over this past week. I am aware of times I did not readily forgive, where I tapped into past hurts and responded in unloving ways. You probably identify with Paul like I do when he says in Romans 7:12, 14-25:

> So then, the law is holy, and the commandment is holy, righteous and good. . . . We know that the law is spiritual; but I am unspiritual, sold as a slave to sin. I do not understand what I do. For what I want to do I do not do, but what I hate I do. And if I do what I do not want to do, I agree that the law is good. As it is, it is no longer I myself who do it, but it is sin living in me. I know that nothing good lives in me, that is, in my sinful nature. For I have the desire to do what is good, but I cannot carry it out. For what I do is not the good I want to do; no, the evil I do not want to do—this I keep on doing. Now if I do what I do not want to do, it is no longer I who do it, but it is sin living in me that does it. So I find this law at work: When I want to do good, evil is right there with me. For in my inner being I delight in God's law; but I see another law at work in the members of my body, waging war against the law of my mind and making me a prisoner of the law of sin at work

within my members. What a wretched man I am! Who will rescue me from this body of death? Thanks be to God—through Jesus Christ our Lord!

Amen! How we must rely on God to live an infinitely better way. I need the Father to talk to, Jesus to imitate, and the Holy Spirit to empower me to live life abundantly for His glory. When the disciples were asked by the Pharisees why Jesus ate with sinners and tax collectors, Jesus said, "It is not the healthy who need a doctor, but the sick" (Matthew 9:12). Aren't you glad that Jesus was concerned about us—sinful and hurting people?

As I close this chapter, I recall one dear surgeon, now retired, as he spoke of the days when he constructed a small box with a string that enabled him to spend hours practicing surgical procedure. He became an exceptional surgeon, with skilled, practiced fingers—a physician you would want addressing your case!

Praise God, He is and has always been the Surgeon we can run to. He never ceases being the Great Physician perfectly familiar with each personal case, unsurpassed in His skill at heart surgery, ready to cut out all that affects the health of our soul. He alone knows everything about each of us.

Praise God for sending Jesus to redeem us from our sinful ways. Thank Him for completely forgiving our obvious transgressions as well as our hidden faults. Imitate Him in forgiving others as we have been forgiven ourselves.

Rx: Freely forgive as you have been forgiven and experience the joy of reconciled relationships.

℞

Chapter 11

Grace and Gratitude

Name : _____   Age : _____

Address : _____   Date : _____

Keep your servant also from willful sins; may they not rule over me. Then I will be blameless, innocent of great transgression.

—Psalm 19:13

Label ☐

Refill 0 1 2 3 4 5 PRN

Refill 0 1 2 3 4 5 PRN

O n several occasions I have been in a courtroom. There is an aura within the building that you can feel immediately upon entering. It is a solemn place, where significant, often life-changing, decisions are made. Respect for the importance of the courtroom and the authority of the judge is apparent. Those present are on their very best behavior.

Picture yourself, for a moment, standing before God as Judge. Scripture tells us that we will face Him one day. We will stand before the only Perfect One. Isaiah reminded the people of Israel, "The LORD takes his place in court; he rises to judge the people" (Isaiah 3:13). Scripture warned the people of God again, "Therefore, O house of Israel, I will judge you, each one according to his ways, declares the Sovereign LORD. Repent! Turn away from all your offenses; then sin will not be your downfall" (Ezekiel 18:30).

Our God "is a God of justice" (Psalm 50:6). He sees every action, knows every thought, and is even aware of our words before they are said. We would not blatantly disrespect the appointed official in an earthly courtroom. How can it be then that we often find it so easy to disregard God—the ultimate, heavenly, perfect Judge? Do we truly comprehend the righteousness of God and tremble in holy fear before Him? Do we live each day in light of knowing that one day we will give an account for how we have lived our lives?

We don't want to be counted among the arrogant who are indifferent to God, rejecting both His truth and His ways. The psalmist asks God for help so that he does not purposely and foolishly choose to disobey the will of the Father, so that he might be found innocent—not guilty—in God's court of law. We should echo this desire and look up to God, who alone makes it possible for us to be blameless. "I lift up my eyes to the hills—where does my help come from? My help comes from the Lord, the Maker of heaven and earth" (Psalm 121:1-2).

The Trials of Life

Our Helper is always there when we call on Him. He gives us everything we need to live righteously for His glory and for our best. There are many different kinds of trials in this life. He is ready, willing, and able to help in each and every one.

Malpractice trials are a heavy burden for our doctor husbands. They work tirelessly to care for each patient to the best of their abilities. Yet, regrettably, there is that rare occasion when there is a bad outcome. This may result in a case being brought against the doctor.

Years ago this happened to my husband, and it was devastating. A child was brought into the emergency room who tragically died shortly thereafter. It was a horrible day for Ed. He carefully did everything he could to save this child, but the parents had waited too long to bring the child in for medical attention and nothing could be done. I can still remember how he looked when he walked in the door, struggling with the huge loss this family endured. In their grief, they decided to pursue a lawsuit, hoping that they could blame someone else for their tragic loss.

God worked in many marvelous ways throughout this process. The first "God thing" came when Ed's lawyer contacted him about settling out of court. He was concerned because the case involved a child and juries are often sympathetic to the loss of a child. After praying, Ed felt led to write the lawyer a letter explaining that he was a follower of Christ and felt he wanted to go to trial because he was innocent. Ed believed that settling would be choosing the easy way out and not really placing his trust fully in God for the outcome of the trial. It also seemed to him to be an admission of guilt. Ed went on to explain that he believed this was what God wanted him to do. The lawyer, who had been appointed by the insurance company, called to say that he was a Christian, too (God's wonderful provision), and totally understood where Ed was coming from.

The trial was a nightmare. Friends cared for our children so that I could be with him on those awful days. Each day I went into the courtroom with him to pray and support Ed as best I could. I found it so difficult to keep my mouth closed when accusations and inferences were directed toward my husband. I knew that Ed had done all he possibly could to save their child, and while the family lashed out at him in anger, he was grieving deeply for them—for the empty spot in their home.

The day Ed took the witness stand was one neither of us will ever forget. It was stressful beyond words to be relentlessly interrogated. Still, Ed remained calm (I was not) and showed great wisdom in his answers to the difficult questions. I later asked him how he remained so composed. He explained that he felt an amazing sense of God's presence and a feeling of being surrounded by angels as he sat in that chair. It was a peace that he knew was supernatural. Isn't that just like God, to intervene as only He can?

After four grueling days of testimony, the jury quickly arrived at a verdict in less than an hour. They clearly recognized Ed's blamelessness and understood that only God could have prevented the child's death that day. It was a relief for Ed to be found not guilty, to have his conviction that he was innocent of the charges confirmed and upheld by the jury. Yet, the ache for this family still remains in our hearts today.

I pray your husband never has to go through this ordeal. However, if he does, he will need your full support, your prayers, and your presence by his side. It is an unfortunate consequence of practicing medicine in our culture. Sometimes the suits are indeed legitimate, many times they are not. Either way, the righteous Judge will be with you and your husband through this tribulation when your focus is on honoring Him.

The relief we experienced when Ed received an "innocent" verdict reminds me of the indescribable liberation we have through a personal relationship with our heavenly Father. This righteous Judge has declared us "not guilty." Not because we deserve it, for we surely do not, but because He willingly and lovingly paid the penalty for all of our sins—the costly price of the life of His Son, Jesus. All the charges brought against you and me have been removed, as though we had never sinned. We are justified and forgiven, with all our sins wiped clean, as if they had never happened. We are declared not guilty! Amazing! How can we not express our deepest gratitude to our awesome, incredibly merciful God?

Walk in His Shoes

Many patients are grateful for the compassionate care our husbands give them. These people are a joy and are a reminder of why he went into medicine—to care for the sick and the suffering. Others, in the stress of their infirmities at the time, may yell loudly or spew harsh words at our husbands. Drug seekers may be angry they are not getting what they came for. People in pain may say unkind things they normally would not. Their anguish may result in them taking it out on the doctor who can't fix the problem fast enough. The list goes on and on.

Our husbands need us to affirm them, to understand their circumstances, to sympathize with their struggles. When he calls to tell you about his day, do you feel bothered? Do you resent him being at the hospital or the office for long hours only to have your precious conversation time gobbled up with more medical talk? It can be hard to listen at those times. This is when we need to look to God for His help to keep us innocent of transgressions. I shudder to think what would come out of my mouth without His insight and aid.

God is so willing to give us everything we need—including timely help! God's Word instructs us, "Therefore, with minds that are alert and fully sober, set your hope on the grace to be brought to you when Jesus Christ is revealed at his coming. As obedient children, do not conform to the evil desires you had when you lived in ignorance. But just as he who called you is holy, so be holy in all you do; for it is written: 'Be holy, because I am holy.' Since you call on a Father who judges each person's work impartially, live out your time as foreigners here in reverent fear" (1 Peter 1:13-17).

The "therefore" leads me to ask what is it there for. When I look at the preceding verses, I find it is a challenge given in light of Jesus' return one day soon. Verse 13 tells me to be mentally alert, disciplined, and focused—wise advice indeed. We are not to give in to what comes naturally, but instead we are to imitate our Savior by being moral, righteous, self-sacrificing, and holy. Verse 17 contains that word "judge" again. We are challenged to have reverent respect for this Judge and live a life set apart for Him. This life will look "strange" to others around us, because it is not of this world.

We must try to put ourselves in our husband's shoes and try to "walk a mile in them." We need to attempt to understand his day, to listen to him, and to let him know how much we appreciate him. One wise friend, married to an obstetrician, shared with me a lesson that she learned the hard way. She often struggled with being disapproving of her husband when he was home. He seemed to spend more and more time at the office, but would call from work to share stories of patients and staff that had really nice things to say about him.

It dawned on her, one evening, that what was happening was that her criticism made him feel like a failure at home, so he was spending more time at work where he was appreciated. She was actually driving him to do the opposite of what she wanted. She asked for his forgiveness of her critical spirit and sought to make their home environment one in which he felt appreciated and encouraged. She was amazed at the transformation in his schedule and in his demeanor. This change made a huge difference for both of them.

The words of Elizabeth Elliott are a helpful challenge to us on this subject. She said, "It is always possible to be thankful for what is given rather than to complain about what is not given. One or the other becomes a habit of life." What is your tendency—to be thankful or to complain? Remember what you choose is habit-forming.

An Attitude of Gratitude

After many years of marriage, my husband shared with me that most men are continually assaulted by Satan with the question, "Am I enough?" Yes, even our high-achieving, seemingly secure men hear this query. How essential it is for us to be aware of this so that we can let him know, in many creative ways, just how wonderful we think he is.

Carrying this a bit further, I deliberately choose to greet my husband cheerfully when he arrives home, letting him know he is vital to me. When I hear his car pull into the garage, I try to think of something funny or uplifting to say when he asks about my day. Then, I am prepared to be positive instead of blurting out something negative or demanding. When he leaves in the morning, I make an effort to occasionally tell him, "Thank you for working so hard for our family, you are such a good provider."

An old saying, "Hem your blessings with thankfulness so they don't unravel," is helpful to keep in your mind and heart. Our family has a notebook that we call our "Attitude of Gratitude Book" in which we record the many stories of God's faithfulness to us. When something occurs that is a "God thing," we write it down. With thankful hearts, we remember to praise God for His goodness. Focusing on the things we have to be thankful for, both past and present, has challenged us to develop attitudes of gratitude for His provision in our lives and His faithful answers to our prayers. Practical, purposeful, and powerful—this focus keeps us looking upward.

Everyone we love and everything we have is a gift from the Lord. Our hearts should overflow with gratitude, not for the gifts, but for the Giver of these precious gifts. It is so easy to be thankful when I am pleased with the gift, but so difficult to have gratitude when there is an aching loss, severe disappointment, and crushed dreams. That is when we must choose to thank Him, knowing He is working all things together for our good (Romans 8:28).

Believe me, I honestly struggle with keeping a consistent mindset of thankfulness to God. More often than not I am a "fair weather" follower of Christ. Oh, how I long to change that. I want to thank God for all things, imitating fellow believers like Mother Teresa, who said, "The best way to show my gratitude to God is to accept everything, even my problems, with joy."

I long to be like Shadrach, Meshach, and Abednego. I want to stand strong and unshaken, confidently proclaiming to God and those firing up the furnaces in my life, "But even if. . ." I desire to be like young Mary, honest about the fearful mystery and immense challenges she faced, yet able to say to the Most High, "My soul glorifies you and rejoices in you." I yearn to face the unknown tomorrows with trust and gratitude. I want to spontaneously sing hymns of praise like Paul and Silas, no matter what kinds of walls confine me.

These heroes of the faith are so inspiring to me. They were just like you and me in their humanity. Yet, their focus was on the spiritual realm. Theirs was not just a "positive thinking" mind-set. Rather, their state of mind came from intimately knowing our almighty God who is in absolute control. It came from believing that they could bring every situation to Him with thankful hearts as they recalled His faithfulness in the past. We have this same God and this same opportunity.

Philippians 4:6-7 encourages us, "in everything, by prayer and petition, with thanksgiving, present your requests to God. And the peace of God, which transcends all understanding, will guard your hearts and your minds in Christ Jesus." Prayer and thanksgiving dramatically change how we view our circumstances. It is imperative that we stay centered on God, with thankful hearts, to be able to minister to our husbands, as well as to others around us. In order to do this, we must also attend to ourselves.

That will look different for each one of us. Find what works for you and be consistent with it. One group shared suggestions that helped them, such as getting enough sleep, planning a date night twice a month, spending time with friends regularly, reading inspiring books, going for a daily walk, working on a favorite hobby, and being involved in a small group with other believers.

We simply must take care of ourselves so that we can care for others. The best way to do this is to rely on our gracious, loving heavenly Father to fill us. Are you familiar with the words of this older song by Annie Johnson Flint? They speak powerfully to me about what God promises to do in my life when there is a need. His plan for your provision will abundantly surpass your request.

> When we have exhausted our store of endurance,
> When our strength has failed ere the day is half done,
> When we reach the end of our hoarded resources,
> Our Father's full giving is only begun.
> His love hath no limit,
> His grace hath no measure,
> His power hath no boundary known unto men,
> For out of His infinite riches in Jesus,
> He giveth, and giveth, and giveth again.

Charles Spurgeon, too, understood our need for God's ever-present help. He wrote, "Jehovah who created all things is equal to every emergency; heaven and earth are at the disposal of Him who made them, therefore, let us be very joyful in our infinite helper." How thankful I am for His boundless aid. I am in great need of my Helper to keep me "innocent of great transgression." I need His filling to keep me in good spiritual health and to allow my resulting "wellness" to impact those around me.

Sickness at the Doctor's House

Most likely, your doctor husband wants to minister to your needs too. This hopefully includes lovingly caring for you when you are well and tenderly attending to your physical needs when you become ill. After all, he specializes in caring for the sick. Be warned, however—he may not care for you in the way you are expecting. He may simply be too busy caring for others. One day this reality hit home hard.

Thankfully, I am seldom ill. But one particular day, I really learned to appreciate my normal good health. I woke up during the night with one of those awful gastrointestinal bugs—the kind that make you feel like you're going to die. I told Ed how bad I felt before he left for the hospital. (Although, my many trips to the bathroom to vomit and . . . well, you know . . . probably had already clued him in.) Of course, the medical community, who should best understand the realities of illness, does not allow doctors to take sick days to care for themselves or an ill wife. Off he went with kind words to pray for me. I really did need those prayers.

The children woke up their usual way—cheerful and full of energy. They were five, three, and one at the time. I literally crawled from my bed and went into the hall to instruct my two older children, Kristi and Kim, that Mommy was ill and would need their help. I managed to stand long enough to get Jon out of his crib and change his diaper. That was the end of my strength. The girls helped Jon down the stairs, and I slowly descended after them, stopping to rest as I crawled down each step.

What happened next startled me. My children, who rarely watched television, looked on in delight as I turned it on, found Sesame Street, and placed a box of Cheerios in front of them. Thankfully, they were thrilled with the novelty of the show and the "picnic" on the floor. I laid down on the couch, attempting to rest, except for my all too frequent trips to the bathroom. God has blessed me with wonderful children who were usually obedient and fun to be around. That day they were especially good, and I was so very grateful.

Not wanting to expose any of my friends to my illness, I didn't call anyone to ask for help. Relatives were states away. My husband was my only hope for rescue. He called late morning to say he would try to get away briefly at noon. I began to dream of returning to my bed to rest, while Ed would bring me ice chips and soothe my fevered brow.

My dear husband did show up at lunchtime. He had a look of concern on his face while his eyes conveyed that he was a man on a mission. The children were thrilled to see Daddy home at lunchtime—a rare treat. They bounced all over him with happiness. Then they assured him that they were taking good care of Mommy.

What happened next is something I will always remember. Ed explained to me that he had fifteen minutes to spare and that he planned to spend it by starting an IV so that I would not get dehydrated. I know he meant well, but only a doctor's wife would be asked to endure such treatment! I weakly tried to protest . . . worrying about the kids seeing me with an IV and wondering how was I going to go to the bathroom with this contraption in, since we had no portable IV pole at home.

He skillfully (and swiftly so the children wouldn't see) inserted the IV needle . . . multiple times . . . with no success. This was most unusual for Ed who was known to successfully start IVs on patients when others could not. Apparently, I was already quite dehydrated, making it very difficult. Alas, soon the fifteen precious minutes were up. He kissed me on the head, gave the children instructions on how to care for Mommy, and went out the door. My hope of being rescued and pampered went out the door too.

Fortunately, my heavenly Father demonstrated His loving care for me in powerful ways that day. The children were really good, caring and praying for me in their own sweet ways. Though I didn't know it, Ed was very concerned and actually arranged to leave early that day to come home and care for me that evening. He must have had to work hard to find others to cover for him. Fortunately, I did recover. I also realized that I needed to change my expectations as a doctor's wife.

You'd think I would have learned that already in the years he'd been involved in a medical career. I should have figured this out when he managed my second labor by phone. He was a third-year family-medicine resident at the time and was at the hospital when my labor began. He informed me that it was not a good time for me to be in labor as he was already "up to his eyeballs caring for women about to have their babies." He asked if I could wait a while. Obviously, he had never been in labor himself!

Fortunately, a dear friend who was also a resident's wife came to pick up our first child, and Ed did have a few minutes to come home for me. Labor slowed once I got to the hospital—of course. Only a doctor's wife would send both her own doctor and her husband to the on-call room to sleep while she walks the halls to stimulate labor— alone.

Sometimes, the role reverses and our care-giving husbands become the ones needing treatment. It has been said that nurses are terrible patients, and the only ones who are worse are doctors. Those of us in medicine, who should know better, are not good patients! Our doctor husbands want to be well *now* to get back to their busy schedules. They often do not follow their own advice to rest when they are ill.

As a result, it can be a real challenge to care for them. At the same time, it is a joy and privilege to do so. We get to attend to the one who typically cares for everyone else. What an opportunity we have, when his busyness is slowed by an illness, to get to spend time with him and to minister to him. It will likely be short-lived.

Sometimes, the compassionate care we need to extend to our husbands may be for emotional or mental health. A wise, new resident's wife recently asked for prayer and advice in being a support to her husband who she sensed was experiencing some signs of depression. The typical feelings of inadequacy during residency, along with other stress factors, were taking their toll on him. This kind wife wanted to help in any way she could.

Our husbands deal with many heavy burdens in life. Endlessly, they see death, suffering, illness, and painful emotional issues up close and personal. They also deal with weighty business issues such as contract disputes with their medical partners, productivity pressures, time demands, and on and on. No wonder they become ill themselves. They do indeed need our tender, loving care.

We can only give this compassionate care when we seek the Giver of all good things. John Owen reminds us, "The duties God requires of us are not in proportion to the strength we possess in ourselves. Rather, they are proportional to the resources available to us in Christ. We do not have the ability in ourselves to accomplish the least of God's tasks."

When illness strikes your family, it is helpful to enjoy the advantages and try to downplay the disadvantages of being a medical wife. In truth, there are huge advantages, such as when, as a toddler, our Jon would walk into our bedroom in the middle of the night and inform me that his ear hurt. He knew Ed would be the one to check his ear, but he also knew that the chances of waking Ed up were slim. It was wonderfully convenient to have Ed there to check him and give the necessary medication and treatment. Ed being able to care for the medical needs of our family was a blessing that occurred countless times. He also had the wisdom to know when it was appropriate to refer a condition to a colleague. Life always has many medical issues and emergencies that occur. It is a gift from the Lord to have a doctor residing in the home!

God has called us to be a doctor's wife just as He has given our husbands the call to be a doctor. They are both high callings. Jesus sent his disciples "out to preach the kingdom of God and to heal the sick" (Luke 9:2). Likewise He has given our husbands this call, with us as the helper beside him. How critical it is to see the vision to serve God together through the ministry of medicine—supporting and encouraging one another in the journey. This joint effort allows God to use our support of our husbands to help them be more effective in healing broken bodies. More importantly, we partner with them in the healing of hurting souls through the ministry of the Gospel.

Working in Tandem

Picture Jesus in the Gospels—our supreme prototype and compassionate Savior! What a treasure it is to be focused on His loving example as we walk alongside our husbands. Working together toward your common goals as you hold each other up and cheer one another on has been His best plan from the beginning of time.

The word "team" comes to mind as I think of how we work together with our husbands for God's glory and our mutual benefit. George MacDonald, mentor of C.S. Lewis, phrased this well. "The highest calling of every husband and wife is to help each other to do the will of God." Psalm 34:3 puts it beautifully, "Glorify the LORD with me; let us exalt his name together."

There is a practical analogy that has helped me better understand the teamwork of our high calling to minister through medicine, to encourage each other in our individual ministries, and in our joint labors for building God's Kingdom. For our twentieth wedding anniversary, Ed and I purchased a tandem bike as a gift to each other. We had been bike riding for years and really enjoyed this activity together. The problem was that we often traveled quite a distance apart because he could get up the hills much faster than I could and would ride ahead due to his stronger legs. We decided to buy a bike that kept us together. What fun this has been!

But what an adjustment it has been, as well, to this new way of riding. One of the first things we learned was the importance of communication. Discussing where we were going and how fast to get there were crucial. Was this a scenic ride or a speed ride? Would we stop or push on to our destination? These and other questions needed to be dialoged about and answered.

Ed and I had to learn how to get on the bike together so that we could begin pedaling at the same time. It took talking to one another and coordinating our efforts just to get started. Then, once we were under way, we quickly learned how important it was for Ed to warn me of hazards ahead or bumps in the road. There are also many "bumps" in the road of life that we need to work together to "pedal" through or overcome. It can be hard work to stay the course together.

A tandem bike can only have one lead biker, with the other biker sitting in the seat behind. At first, this was uncomfortable for me to not be steering (to not have control!) and to not see all that was directly in front of us. I learned to trust Ed to lead us, to be the one responsible for the road ahead. I began to relax and enjoy the scenery along the way as I relinquished this role to Ed both on our bike and in our marriage. What joy we experience in reaching our destination together! We are often rewarded with a beautiful view and a fulfilling sense of accomplishment.

In the same way, as couples we need to learn how to work in tandem—to discuss our plans, where we are heading, and when and how to get there. We must be committed to working together to reach our common goals. We must encourage one another when the road looks long and difficult.

Just as we needed to maintain our bike with regular tune-ups, we also need to care for our marriage by making it a priority to keep it "well tuned." Scheduling meaningful time together, praying together regularly, sharing emotional and physical intimacy, keeping our relationship up-to-date—including resolving conflict—are critical for the health of our marriages.

You will find there are many opportunities to work in tandem for the good of building God's kingdom. Several months ago, Ed and I spent a Sunday afternoon doing something very rewarding together. We, along with one hundred other people from our community of churches, worked side by side to assemble 40,000 meals for Stop Hunger Now. These meals were going to feed earthquake victims in Haiti as well as families in need in the Ivory Coast. How I love serving the Lord together with my husband. Don't you, too?

As Steve Green so powerfully expresses in song, "May those who come behind us find us faithful." May we serve beside our husband and beside one another for the glory of our God!

Help Along the Way

We really do need each other on this journey, don't we? Scripture encourages both the young and those who are no longer young to be examples, to be encouragers to those around them. I hope that as you have read, you have begun to feel a sense of camaraderie and support in the issues you face as the spouse of someone in the medical field.

A friend recently e-mailed me to ask for advice on an issue that was troubling her. Her words caught me by surprise when she said, "So I kept thinking about who I could go to for wisdom, and of course that led me straight to you!" Any wisdom I have comes from God and His Word, from the life experiences He has chosen for me, from the lessons I have learned from many mistakes I have made, and from the many sensible people He has placed in my path.

Jeremiah reminds us, "This is what the LORD says: 'Let not the wise boast of their wisdom or the strong boast of their strength or the rich boast of their riches, but let the one who boasts boast about this: that they have the understanding to know me, that I am the LORD, who exercises kindness, justice and righteousness on earth, for in these I delight,' declares the LORD" (Jeremiah 9:23-24). This is the wisdom I desire, to know Him more fully each day.

My heart truly desires to be the woman God desires me to be. Titus says, "Likewise, teach the older women to be reverent in the way they live, not to be slanderers or addicted to much wine, but to teach what is good. Then they can train the younger women to love their husbands and children, to be self-controlled and pure, to be busy at home, to be kind, and to be subject to their husbands, so that no one will malign the word of God" (Titus 2:3-5).

That is quite a charge to us as women! It still seems strange to me to be seen as an "older woman," but each of us has someone we can learn from. Likewise, we all also have younger women we can teach. I want to promote whole-hearted love for your husband and your children and cheer you on in passing this on to other women. God's ways bring sweet harmony to our homes.

Do you recall the lovely quote from *Stepping Heavenward* about how things used to be when married to a doctor in 1869? Remember the line, "not quite as much honey in the honeymoon as was expected"? There is a paragraph towards the end of the book that addresses this concept of harmony in our home.

Happiness, in other words love, in married life is not a mere accident. When the union has been formed, as most Christian unions are, by God Himself, it is His intention and His will that it shall prove the unspeakable joy of both husband and wife, and become more and more so from year to year. But we are imperfect creatures, wayward and foolish as little children, horribly unreasonable, selfish, and willful. We are not capable of enduring the shock of finding at every turn that our idol is made of clay, and that it is prone to tumble off its pedestal and lie in the dust, till we pick it up and set it in its place again. I was struck with Ernest's asking in the very first prayer he offered in my presence, after our marriage, that God would help us love each other; I felt that love was the very foundation on which I was built, and that there was no danger that I would ever fall short in giving to my husband all he wanted, in full measure. But as he went on day after day repeating this prayer, and I naturally made it with him, I came to see that this most precious of earthly blessings had been and must be God's gift, and that while we both looked at it in that light, and felt our dependence on Him for it, we might safely encounter together all the assaults made upon us by the world, the flesh, and the Devil. I believe we owe it to this constant prayer that we have loved each other so uniformly and with such growing comfort in each other; so that our little discords have always ended in fresh accord, and our love has felt conscious of resting on a rock—and that rock was the will of God."

In our desire to be set apart for the service of our heavenly Father, let us lovingly inspire one another to be godly servants who do not knowingly and willfully sin against our God. Let us come with thankful hearts as we ask for and receive forgiveness of our transgressions. Let us challenge one another to live this life blamelessly before our perfect Judge, as we rely on Him alone for our innocence.

Rx: The Righteous Judge has declared you "not guilty." Express gratitude by giving grace to and serving others as you work in tandem with your husband.

R_X

Chapter 12

Walking with God

Name : _____ Age : _____

Address : _____ Date : _____

May the words of my mouth and the meditation of my heart be pleasing in your sight, O LORD, my Rock and my Redeemer.

—Psalm 19:14

Label ☐

Refill 0 1 2 3 4 5 PRN

Refill 0 1 2 3 4 5 PRN

O n January 12, 2009, an unlikely event occurred on a routine flight out of New York City. Many of us watched in disbelief as we saw the improbable pictures on the news of an airplane that landed on the icy waters of the Hudson River that day. We were amazed as we heard of the superior skill of the pilot and reflected on the supernatural mercy of God.

A CMDA (Christian Medical and Dental Associations) medical student, Andrew Jamison, was on that flight, returning from an internship interview. In his book, *In The Unlikely Event of a Water Landing,* he tells of his thoughts in those last frightening moments as the plane was plunging toward the frigid water. They were thoughts about life and death. Thoughts about God. This was a rare opportunity, especially for a young person, to contemplate his life as it quickly passed before his eyes.

That experience would be life changing for most of us. Such a critical moment forces us to concentrate on what we truly believe and what really matters the most to us. Of course, we need to realistically look at our lives in non-crisis moments too, to assess if the way we are living is consistent with what we believe. Do we say we know God and want to love and serve Him? What are we meditating on or thinking about? Do our words and actions confirm that we are living to please our heavenly Father?

Now, as we consider the final verse of Psalm 19, the psalmist invites us, by example, to examine our own words and the unspoken thoughts of our hearts to see if they might be acceptable to our Lord. He challenges us, in light of God's revelation through His creation and through His Law, to respond by striving to honor our great God with all of our being—including our thoughts, our behaviors, and our speech. We are challenged to speak words worthy of a redeemed creature of God, Yahweh, our Rock, our Redeemer.

A thorough examination is critical for assessing the health of our spiritual life, just as the examination of a patient is necessary to assess their physical health. Throughout Scripture, God carefully addresses the importance of examining our words in order to accurately evaluate the condition of our hearts.

Words of Grace

An excellent example is found in Ephesians 4:29. "Do not let any unwholesome talk come out of your mouths, but only what is helpful for building others up according to their needs, that it may benefit those who listen." Consider the guidance of this verse, as it challenges us to go beyond *doing* good, to also *speaking* what is good.

What does God consider "unwholesome talk"? Surely, this would include bad language, malicious gossip, and slander, among other things. These rotten words injure others and cause division among people. They do not build people up; instead these words tear them down.

At the same time, we are to make sure that the words we do speak are a benefit and a blessing—not only to the person we are speaking to, but also to those within listening range. Wow. Only God can make it possible for our everyday conversations to bless others and demonstrate grace to them.

This grace can only be extended to others when we truly understand the grace God has personally given to each one of us. You may be familiar with the following acronym for grace: God's Riches At Christ's Expense. Ephesians 1:7-8 says it this way, "In him we have redemption through his blood, the forgiveness of sins, in accordance with the riches of God's grace that he lavished on us."

Our awesome God, willingly and lovingly, gave us redemption through Jesus' sacrifice. We did not deserve this merciful favor. We cannot earn it. We simply receive it through faith because of His grace. Let this truth sink in and I think you will agree that it motivates us to want to extend words of kindness and understanding, even if we must turn the other cheek, as we are deeply touched by the grace we have personally received.

When we truly comprehend His grace, the desire grows to love and serve God out of the overflow of what He has poured into our hearts. It is not "works" we have to do, but rather wanting to do what pleases Him as a response from our grateful heart.

We are also led to share this blessing of unmerited favor with others who do not know the Lord. "Let your conversation be always full of grace, seasoned with salt, so that you may know how to answer everyone" (Colossians 4:6). When we tell others about Christ, we want to share in a respectful and graceful way. We want our words to be "tasty" to allow further dialogue.

This is also particularly good advice for everyday discussions within our own homes. This verse has often reminded me to be purposeful about talking with family members in a way that builds relationships with them. The fruit of this mind-set is sweet. How blessed I am to have been given the gift of my two daughters, Kristi and Kim. It has been a joy to raise them and share life with them. They have grown into godly young women that I am so proud of and that I consider to be among my best friends. Oh, how I have loved having sweet conversations with them over the years!

I have also treasured the privilege of meeting with the young women in my Side by Side Bible study group. Their transparency and teachable hearts make our times together so rich. These ladies do not come to the meeting with masks on, but are real and honest about their lives. These sweet women are both sisters and daughters to me—a true gift from God.

The practical use of timely, humble, pleasing, and carefully chosen words is so important to preserve our relationships and honor God. One example in my own life of this principle at work is my "sock story."

My husband was blessed with one of those mothers who was very efficient at running a home. As a child, he would get dressed in the morning and drop his pajamas onto the floor. Miraculously, when he got ready for bed that night, those same pajamas were washed, ironed, folded, and back in his drawer.

Fast forward to being married to me and living in our home. He naturally assumed that this is what would continue to happen to his clothes after they ended up on the floor. It took me a while to realize that he was not trying to make more work for me, he was just truly oblivious to the fact that not picking up his clothes meant I would need to. One day it occurred to me that I needed to speak with him about this habit, which was building resentment in me.

First, I needed to talk with God about this issue. That was perhaps the hardest part, as He worked on me for several weeks until my heart was ready to talk to Ed in a way that honored both my husband and my God. I lovingly approached Ed and said, "I have been picking up your socks for a while now. I just want you to know that I love you and I am truly willing to continue to pick up your socks and serve you in this way. I also want you to know that taking the time to pick up after you means that I will have less time to do other things, including less time to spend with you. I would like you to think about which you would prefer—to have me continue to pick up your socks or for you to put your things away yourself, allowing us to have more time together."

He had not even realized that I was doing this task or that it required time to do so. His response was amazing. Right away he said that he had not realized what he was doing and that he certainly would prefer that we have more time together. To this day, I have not needed to pick up his clothes. We brainstormed together and came up with a convenient hamper for dirty items and hooks in the closet for the items he wanted to wear again, but did not want to put away. What a great system. A win-win for both of us.

What made the difference, I am convinced, is that I went to him with a right heart and sweet words (both made possible only by God). I believe I would still be resenting his habit and still be picking up after him if I had spoken to him with the words and the attitude I initially felt. This anecdote was so helpful to remember in other similar situations in our marriage. Yes, seeking to do things God's way is surely far superior to what comes naturally to me.

I am far from perfect. I make many mistakes. Pleasing God with my words is my sincere desire, yet I am too often tempted to say things without thinking. Fortunately, God's Word is full of remedies for my malady. Resisting the natural urge to control others allows grace to flow more freely. Extending grace to those who do not deserve it is modeling Jesus' way. Refusing to compare ourselves to others to see if we measure up is freeing to our souls.

Donald Barnhouse, the late Bible scholar and pastor, defined grace well with these words: "Love that goes upward is worship; love that goes outward is affection; love that stoops is grace." Are there people in your life that you could "stoop" for and show unexpected kindness to? Could your husband be one of those in need of this unmerited favor? 1 Peter 4:8 instructs us, "Above all, love each other deeply, because love covers over a multitude of sins."

Does life feel overwhelming to you at times, making it hard for you to think about giving others compassion when you feel so needy yourself? Paul has good advice for us concerning this dilemma in 2 Corinthians 12:9-10. He had a "thorn in his flesh" that was tormenting him, so he asked the Lord to remove it. God's reply to Paul was, "My grace is sufficient for you, for my power is made perfect in weakness." Paul goes on to exclaim, "Therefore I will boast all the more gladly about my weaknesses, so that Christ's power may rest on me. That is why, for Christ's sake, I delight in weaknesses, in insults, in hardships, in persecutions, in difficulties. For when I am weak, then I am strong." A profound paradox, indeed. When we are weak, we recognize our need to run to our strong God. As we depend on Him, we are strong in His strength. Why? Because His grace is more than sufficient for our every need. He can enable us to extend His grace to others even when we don't "feel" like it.

Careful Communication

Sam Keen said, "We come to love not by finding a perfect person, but by learning to see an imperfect person perfectly." I like this idea of my life companion seeing me this way! I really want to show him grace and view him this way too. I want to be quick to overlook minor offenses and slow to let words escape from my mouth, so that I can filter out the unwholesome ones.

In marriage, hurtful words can come from selfishness, disrespect, taking each other for granted, stubbornness, or wanting the other person to change. We forget the common courtesies like "please" and "thank you" that we used to say to one another. We have long forgotten the compliments that flowed so freely when we dated.

Practically speaking, as I often suggest to women I am counseling, make a list of traits you really like about your man. Be sure to do this when you are delighted with him. Add to this list, as time goes on, all the qualities that you appreciate about him. Then, when you are feeling upset with him, read this list. It will put that one fault in perspective as you focus on the many things that he is doing right. Remembering the positives and overlooking the annoyances is grace in action.

Speaking our concerns in the form of a "sandwich" is particularly helpful. My husband has often expressed that it is so beneficial to hear something he is doing well first, then a concern (in the middle of the sandwich) and, at the end of the conversation, another affirmation.

For example, I may be tempted to blurt out, "This chicken is undercooked—gross." (Perhaps a true statement, but not edifying words.) But instead I will try to say something like, "I appreciate that you like to grill food for us. You do a great job, and I really like having your help with our meal. It seems to me that this chicken is a little undercooked. I would prefer next time, that mine be cooked a little longer. Thank you for listening to my request. You are indeed the 'grill master' (a name affectionately given to Ed by our granddaughter)." This takes a little more thought and a few more words, but his response has convinced me that this approach is well worth the time and effort.

Communication is so very important in a marriage. We need to study our spouse to know how to communicate in their language. This is not just through our words, but also our tone and body language.

I taught childbirth classes for ten years and loved this wonderful time preparing couples for the arrival of their little ones. But I was astounded to learn, in a seminar taken in preparation for my teaching, that people only remember 10 percent of what you say. That made me really consider how I chose my words, what my tone was, how much I involved them in the conversation, how much hands-on teaching I did, and how many stories I should tell to illustrate a point.

Lack of communication causes great strain on our marriages. Most of us know this first hand. There are many good books to give you insight in this crucial area. One excellent resource is *Communication: Key to Your Marriage* by H. Norman Wright. The author challenges us with these words, "The companionship and completeness that God intended in our marriage grow out of communication as two people share each day and the meaning of their lives."

As Dwight Small says, "The heart of marriage is its communication system. . . . But no couple begins marriage with highly developed communication. It is not something they bring into marriage ready made but something to be continually cultivated through all the experiences of their shared life. Satisfying companionship and a sense of completeness develop as husband and wife learn to communicate with openness and understanding."

Deep, honest communication is essential to a healthy marriage. We all know that, yet somehow we expect it to just happen naturally.

We don't think to invest our time and effort, even though we realize all the other skills and successes we have obtained in life have required our commitment and hard work to be accomplished.

In our marriage, Ed and I have found it to be very beneficial to address the "wedge" between us, as opposed to labeling the "problem" as being the other person. When we identify some issue that seems to be distancing us from one another (the wedge), we try to focus our efforts on constructive co-labor to resolve the source of disharmony. This helps us feel as though we are working together, with God's guidance, to tear down the walls that try to come between us. We waste so much time and do so much damage when we try to point fingers and make the issue the other person.

An example of how this can work came from a friend who found herself constantly disappointed that her physician husband was missing many important occasions. Together, they addressed this "wedge" between them and came up with some good ideas. He really made an effort to let her know his plans as he saw them unfolding at work, so that she would have a more realistic picture of his schedule. At the same time, she made a conscious effort to change her thinking and expectations, so that she was not constantly disappointed and frustrated. Then she was delighted when he was able to participate.

Love and Respect

Understanding our differences as men and women is essential for the well being of our relationships. *Love and Respect,* by Emerson Eggerichs, is a valuable resource that teaches from a biblical perspective about the ways husbands and wives are dissimilar. He shares how we often react negatively toward one another because we do not understand the impact of the woman's driving need to feel loved and the man's driving need to feel respected.

This concept helped Ed and I, in hindsight, to understand a conflict we once had in the middle of the night. We were sleeping soundly when we heard a loud crash that came from the bathroom. Startled, we both jumped up to see what it was. Apparently, the shower caddy had come undone and fallen to the floor, spilling the heavy shampoo bottles that were inside. I had just found this caddy the day before and put it up. I was so proud of my "find" and the way this gadget attached to the shower wall—it had the usual suction cups, but also a clever system to lock them into place so it would not come loose. Well, obviously that didn't work out very well!

But being the helpful wife that I am, I explained to my very handy husband how to reinstall the caddy. He was quite offended as he heard, "You are too stupid to figure out how to fix this by yourself." Of course, I did not say those words, nor was I thinking them, but he felt them.

I was offended by his harsh tone. I thought I was being so helpful because I had read the directions and didn't think he would know how this new suction system worked. I remember thinking, *How can he be so unloving toward me when I am just trying to be helpful?* He did not realize how his tone affected me.

We were both hurt and not understanding one another. It was a long night until we were able to resolve the issue and forgive each other. How helpful it is now that we better understand that God has made us with different needs. We have worked hard to improve our listening skills to seek to comprehend what the other person is really saying and to communicate in a way that enables the other person to truly hear our words in their own language.

One of my favorite Eggerichs quotes is, "In the ultimate sense, your marriage has nothing to do with your spouse. It has everything to do with your relationship to Jesus Christ." This is a wise and convicting truth that God continues to use in my life. Remember, Psalm 19:14 encourages us to be sure that our words are pleasing to Him. If those phrases that escape our lips are based on our vibrant relationship with Jesus, they will indeed be sweet, edifying words.

I can easily allow frustration to be vented at my husband simply because I get off track in my own life. It does not have anything to do with him, but he may be the recipient of my unkind words. Primarily this comes from neglecting my spiritual life. After many years of experience, I recognize the symptoms now. Particularly when I begin to see our relationship in a negative light and, of course, assume it is my husband's fault.

Keep Your House in Order

An analogy that has been helpful to me in understanding my relationship with God and my husband is to imagine how an airplane is flown. Picture with me the roles of those involved—the pilot is the main one in charge, the boss, the wise and experienced one. This would be like God. He should be the One that I allow to fly my "plane." The co-pilot listens to the pilot and assists him in the flight. He sometimes takes over the steering, but the control is always under the authority and supervision of the pilot. The co-pilot would represent my husband. Finally, the navigator is an important person whose input should be listened to as this person has studied the route and is aware of factors that influence the journey. This illustrates me, the wife. Each role is essential and complementary, playing its part to ensure that the plane gets safely to its destination.

Taking this analogy a step further, think for a minute about your children—whether your home is blessed with them now or at some time in the future. They are like the passengers on the plane. They are protected and cared for, while at the same time they are expected to behave in certain safe ways so that the rest of the crew can do their jobs.

Unfortunately, sometimes the roles of your "crew" can get mixed up. Be warned there could be a possible crash ahead! There have been times when I have been tempted to put my children before my husband, especially when they were young and they literally screamed for attention. Caution! Do not let your home become a child-centered home. It needs to be primarily a God-centered home and secondarily, a couple-centered home for the good of your entire family. This is God's good plan. The passengers do not tell the pilot or co-pilot or navigator what to do—they do not have control of the airplane, or the home.

There are many benefits of keeping the right priorities in the home. What a life skill you will teach your children when they learn that the world does not revolve around them. We ought to teach them to be "givers," not "takers." We should model this Christ-like quality by involving our children in serving neighbors and friends. Perhaps they could help you with meals or childcare or chores for those in need. A purposeful mind-set to instruct them will remind you to keep godly roles in your home and not be lulled into allowing your children to tell you how things should be run in your home.

Speaking of running a home, this is one area that I have often felt the need for practical advice. After many years of trying to keep my home organized and clean enough for us to live in, to my dismay

I realized that my home was running me. I was not the one in control—I found I was a slave to what needed to be done and felt constantly behind.

I knew I could not possibly expect to keep my home organized and presentable at all times. Yet, we frequently had guests in our home and I could not "crisis clean" before each visit. Also, many of those that came were unexpected. I do believe that a smile and warm greeting meant much more to our guests than the cleanliness of my home, but there is a balance. Mine was dizzyingly off. I needed a new, wise plan.

This is an area where seeking advice and suggestions from others can be so helpful, for we can learn so much from each other! But I finally found a system that put me back in control and has worked well for me for many years. First I divided the rooms of my home among the months of the year. Then I set aside one day a month to really clean thoroughly—the "deep" cleaning as some refer to it— whatever room or rooms were designated for that month. Since I knew this rotated, I chose to overlook some other rooms saying, "This is not your month." Then I spent only a few hours each week doing the basic maintenance of dusting and vacuuming and bathrooms.

Teaching the children and Ed, by example, to pick up and put away our messes at the end of the day helped so much as neatness looks "clean"—even if it is not. We all have different standards of cleanliness and different personalities. Find what works well for you and your family and commit to that plan. You will love feeling in control of your home (most of the time) and enjoy the freedom of focusing more energy on those who live in and visit your home.

What do you observe in other women's habits as you watch them manage meal times? We all seem to come with kitchen strengths and weaknesses from our past, don't we? I have always loved to cook and am thankful for this as cooking is a significant part of what we do. If you do not like to cook, be thankful for all the healthy convenience foods available to assist us today in this task. Organization is key to whatever method you use. Thinking about ingredients and thawing foods early in the day aid greatly in reducing anxiety during that time of day when everyone is asking, "What's for dinner?" Slow cookers are wonderful. They do necessitate planning ahead, but the reward is a nourishing, tasty meal that requires much less effort in the long run. An added benefit is that they can easily keep dinner warm if your husband is running late!

Finding practical ways to more efficiently run our homes and making sure we keep our priorities in order can make all the difference in keeping our lives on course. Our God is a God of order and He wants us to have joy abundantly in this life, despite the brokenness and mistakes that surround us. We can break the bondage of the past and make the present honoring to Him, with His divine help. We can truly thrive and not just survive in this life as a doctor's wife.

Walk in His Way

Most of us love the adventure of a journey and the anticipation of a refreshing vacation—at least once all the hard work of planning and packing are done. One of our favorite escapades came when our family had the wonderful opportunity to experience a six-week cross-country trip. Ed was able to get the extended time off by working extra shifts before and after our excursion. Though it made those months leading up to our vacation and afterward more difficult, Ed felt it was worth every moment of the sacrifice for the shared joyful memories we made on that trip.

Our children were twelve, ten, and eight years old at the time (we had not yet adopted our two youngest sons). The beloved pop-up camper again made more special memories of family times together. How blessed we were to enjoy God's creation up close on our adventures. That trip, though taken many years ago, is still talked about with enthusiasm as we recount the amazing sights we saw and the many wonderful times we shared.

I hope you have sensed many of these feelings as I have shared what the Lord has done in my life. You may have experienced some majestic mountain highs and some below sea-level lows as God spoke to your heart. You may have heard just what you needed to hear. Thank you for allowing me to share my life and to be a part of yours as we walk this journey together as pilgrims. Certainly, there have been times I have no longer wanted to walk. After the death of my precious Jon, I no longer wanted to write—not even one word. It took me many months and God's gentle nudging to draw me back to writing.

It has been a gift of healing in this long process of grief to pen words to you. Visualizing your busy life and your need for spiritual encouragement has been my motivation. Recounting God's faithfulness has ministered to my own soul as I have told of His supernatural touch on my life and in the lives of people all around me. Let us continue to allow Him to write His narratives on our lives. There are many tales yet to tell.

What has your journey been like? We must never forget that God is with us each step of the way. He comforts us in Jeremiah 29:11-13 with these words: "'For I know the plans I have for you,' declares the LORD, 'plans to prosper you and not to harm you, plans to give you hope and a future. Then you will call on me and come and pray to me, and I will listen to you. You will seek me and find me when you seek me with all your heart.'"

The Bible tell us, "It's in Christ that we find out who we are and what we are living for. Long before we first heard of Christ and got our hopes up, he had his eye on us, had designs on us for glorious living, part of the overall purpose he is working out in everything and everyone" (Ephesians 1:11-12 msg). The question of who we are was so well addressed in a message given by Dr. Gene Rudd, senior vice president of CMDA, at a local fellowship event. This godly doctor challenged those of us in the audience to change the question from "Who are we?" to "Whose are we?" when contemplating the deep meaning of life. We are His. That answer makes all the difference.

Rick Warren, in his life-transforming book, *The Purpose-Driven Life,* puts us in our rightful place in the opening sentences: "It's not about you. The purpose of your life is far greater than your own personal fulfillment, your peace of mind, or even your happiness. It's far greater than your family, your career, or even your wildest dreams and ambitions. If you want to know why you were placed on this planet, you must begin with God. You were born by his purpose and for his purpose."

Some who have traveled before us seem to have understood what this life passage is all about. One of those individuals is mentioned in Genesis 5:24 in a peculiar verse: "Enoch walked with God; then he was no more, because God took him away." Hebrews 11:5 sheds a little more light on this man, "By faith Enoch was taken from this life, so that he did not experience death; he could not be found, because God had taken him away. For before he was taken, he was commended as one who pleased God." Amazing!

Wouldn't you love to have the phrase "she walked with God" be used to describe you? We can walk in God's steps as He shows us the footpath. I love the phrase "walk" as I can visualize the blessings of slowing down to enjoy His presence beside me. I want to allow Him to point out the best way to go, to reveal sights along the way, and to illuminate the dangers that may be encountered. I can almost feel him carrying me at times, too, when I do not have the strength to go on. In the dark times, He even lights my way. "Your word is a lamp for my feet, and a light for my path" (Psalm 119:105).

"The path of the righteous is level; you, the upright One, make the way of the righteous smooth. Yes, LORD, walking in the way of your laws, we wait for you; your name and renown are the desire of our hearts" (Isaiah 26:7-8). It is not easy to do God's will, but He promises to make a smooth way for those who follow Him—those whose desire is to fix their eyes on Him, to please Him, to glorify Him.

Your path may not always seem smooth, but you have your forever faithful Companion there to comfort and guide you as you live for His glory. We can say with David, "You have made known to me the path of life; you will fill me with joy in your presence with eternal pleasures at your right hand" (Psalm 16:11).

He gives us purpose, provision, and perseverance for the journey. Add to that list His amazing promises, such as, "You will keep in perfect peace him whose mind is steadfast, because he trusts in you" (Isaiah 26:3). Another assurance comes from Isaiah 48:17-18 which says, "This is what the LORD says—your Redeemer, the Holy One of Israel: 'I am the LORD your God, who teaches you what is best for you, who directs you in the way you should go. If only you had paid attention to my commands, your peace would have been like a river, your well-being like the waves of the sea."

The benefits of relying on God are countless. One of them is "perfect peace." Sounds wonderful, doesn't it? That is the part that God brings. Our part is to make a choice to believe Him, to place our life in His competent hands, and to stay centered on Him in all circumstances. Isaiah 30:21 reminds us to heed God's correction through His Word and His Holy Spirit to get back on the narrow path, "This is the way; walk in it." We must be willing to follow where He leads, fully trusting in who He is.

Take Up Your Cross

Jesus said, "Whoever wants to be my disciple must deny themselves and take up their cross daily and follow me" (Luke 9:23). He makes it very clear that we have to refuse to give in to our own will, instead pursuing God's will. We must choose to live each day for Christ's sake, not our own.

Oh, how I struggle with my own nature. That sinful woman in me thinks I know the best way to travel this road of life. Oswald Chambers reminds me, "The essence of sin is my claim to my right to myself." I must surrender my assertion to run my own life to the One who created me and knows what is best for me.

My soul longs to fully yield to Jesus, to all He has for me, as He beckons me to follow Him. How about you? Hebrews says, "Let us run with perseverance the race marked out for us, fixing our eyes on Jesus, the pioneer and perfecter of faith" (Hebrews 12:1-2). We will stumble if we look to ourselves or to our circumstances. This walk is not about the amount of our faith in the journey. Instead it is about the *object* of our faith.

I sincerely pray that my written words have been pleasing in the sight of My Rock, My Redeemer. I pray they have blessed you and uplifted you. I hope, like me, you will pray Psalm 139:23-24, "Search me, O God, and know my heart; test me and know my anxious thoughts. See if there is any offensive way in me, and lead me in the way everlasting." Let us allow God to reveal our sin, to lead us to repentance, and to empower us to please Him with our lives. May the "words of our mouth" and the "meditation of our hearts" be acceptable to our awesome Creator. May our unshaken devotion to the only trustworthy One delight His heart.

The abundant blessings of walking in His ways lie ahead. Let's imagine together what this precious path will produce as we trust and obey. May we encourage one another to keep our focus steadfast on pleasing our Lord. Let us no longer run from Him, but to Him. Let us spend no more time turning away from our husband, but instead spend time drawing closer beside him. Join me as we step out in faith and whole-heartedly follow Our Creator, Our Redeemer, Our God. To Him be the glory for ever and ever! Amen.

Rx: Seek to walk in the footsteps of Jesus and follow Him wholeheartedly on the path of your life.

Study Guide

Chapter 1 – Seek the Creator

1. What about God's creation, big or small, amazes you the most? When was the last time you stopped and looked at the world around you with eyes wide open?

2. When did you first become aware of the brokenness of sin in your life and your need for a Savior?

3. Read John 3:16. How is Jesus God's gift to us? What happens when we believe and accept this free gift?

4. What difference has it made to you to know that you are a daughter of the King? Personally? In your family? With your friends? In your marriage?

5. Henry Blackaby once said, "God pursues a continuing love relationship with you that is real and personal." How does this make you feel?

6. Read Mark 16:15. In what ways are you sharing your faith with others?

7. Do others watching you know that you have Jesus in your life? Is it evident in what you say and do at home? In your community?

8. Read Philippians 4:19. What does God say about meeting our needs in this verse? Do you look to your husband to meet needs that only God can meet? What can you do to refocus your attention on God as your source?

9. What does Matthew 6:32-33 tell us about our Father and what He desires for us to seek?

10. What one aspect of your life are you willing to change to begin to apply Ephesians 4:22-24 to your life as a medical spouse?

Chapter 2 – The Mind Matters

1. What causes resentment for you as a medical spouse?

2. How do you express that resentment? (Moodiness, moping, whining, internalizing, temper tantrums?)

3. Who is being affected by your bitterness?

4. How did the following Bible characters handle their resentment?

    Hannah (I Samuel 1:1-18):

    Joseph (Matthew 1:18-25):

    Job (1:13-22, 2:7-10):

    30·31   14-
5. What do Ephesians 4:31 and Hebrews 12:15 say about anger and bitterness?

6. How do we surrender our unmet expectations to God?

7. Romans 12:2 says, "Do not conform any longer to the pattern of this world, but be transformed by the renewing of your mind." What is your mind set on? In what areas do you see a need to renew your mind?

8. God gave His Son to make this new life possible. Only He knows what is best for us. How do we joyfully let Him transform us?

9. Romans 8:5 tells us that "Those who live according to the sinful nature have their minds set on what that nature desires: but those who live in accordance with the Spirit have their minds set on what the Spirit desires." In what ways are you setting your mind on the things of the Spirit?

10. Read Colossians 3:2 and Ephesians 4:22-24. What do these verses say about how we set our minds on what the Spirit desires?

11. What one step can you make to apply these verses in your life?

Chapter 3 – In Pursuit of Wisdom

1. What changes are the most difficult for you? How can you prepare yourself in advance to cope positively with these difficulties?

2. What creative ways can help you to connect more with your husband?

3. Read Proverbs 31:10-12. How do we seek to bring our husbands good and not harm? Share some practical ideas for "bringing him good."

4. What does the wise woman do in Proverbs 14:1? What does the foolish one do? What are some ways a woman can "build her house"?

5. Read Ephesians 4:29. How does applying this verse help our homes to have the fragrant "aroma of Christ" (2 Corinthians 2:14-16)?

6. Proverbs 31:26 describes the noble woman, saying, "She speaks with wisdom, and faithful instruction is on her tongue." What does a woman who speaks with wisdom sound like?

7. "When words are many, sin is not absent, but he who holds his tongue is wise" (Proverbs 10:19). What does this Scripture teach us?

8. James 1:26 tells us, "If anyone considers himself religious and yet does not keep a tight rein on his tongue, he deceives himself and his religion is worthless." What does it mean for us to keep a "tight rein" on our tongue?

9. Think back over the use of your tongue this past week. When is it the hardest for you to control your tongue? Are there changes you would like to make to be wise in the use of your words?

10. Take time to thank God for His Word—His love letter to us—that includes statutes and laws to guide us, for our good and the good of others around us.

Chapter 4 – Maximize the Moment

1. In what ways are you feeling pressure to conform to the expectations of the world around you? Is there an area you believe God wants you to let go of or change?

2. Pastor and author Eugene Peterson states "Busyness is an enemy of spirituality. It is essentially laziness. It is doing the easy thing instead of the hard thing. It is filling our time with our own actions instead of paying attention to God's actions." Do you agree or disagree? Why?

3. How are things going in "building" your home . . . specifically in the area of your relationship with your husband? What changes will help you to experience, or enhance, the heartfelt joy God intends for us?

4. Read Genesis 2:18 and Ecclesiastes 4:9-10. What do these verses say to you about your desire and your need to spend time with your spouse?

5. What are some creative ways to plan time in the week to be with your husband? How can you minimize the time obstacles and maximize your time together?

6. Read Proverbs 18:21a, 19:13b, 21:9. What do these Scriptures tell us that shed some light on how and when to bring up issues?

7. What do Ecclesiastes 3:17 and 10:12 teach us about the importance of the timing of our words?

8. James 4:1 asks, "What causes fights and quarrels among you? Don't they come from your desires that battle within you?" How can this verse help you discern the issues that you need to bring to God to deal with and those that are appropriate to talk with your husband about?

9. Read John 15:9-11. What do these verses tell us about obeying God's commands, His precepts, and the effect this has on our joy?

10. Read Romans 12:9-21. Pick out one verse (from this call to love others) to memorize and apply to your life in regard to your husband. Share why you chose this verse.

Chapter 5 – A Light unto Your Path

1. Read Matthew 6:19-24. What does this passage teach us about the connection between our heart and our treasure (v.21)? What does our attitude toward money reveal about our relationship with God and our commitment to His priorities?

2. Read Matthew 6:25-34. What does this passage remind us of concerning worrying about money? How do we reflect the attitude of "seek first His Kingdom and His righteousness" (verse 33) in our daily lives?

3. What does God love about a "cheerful giver" as mentioned in 2 Corinthians 9:7?

4. Read 1Timothy 6:8-11 and 17-19. What are we to flee? What are we to pursue? Share a practical way to apply a verse from this passage to your life.

5. Spend time alone with God and then with your husband to pray about how you are using your time, your talents, and your finances. Discuss any changes you may feel led to make.

6. 1 John 5:14-15 says, "This is the confidence we have in approaching God: that if we ask anything according to his will, he hears us. And if we know that he hears us—whatever we ask—we know that we have what we have asked of him." What does this verse teach about seeking God's will (not demanding our own will) when we pray?

7. Colossians 4:2 (AMP) says, "Be earnest and unwearied and steadfast in your prayer (life), being (both) alert and intent (in your praying) with thanksgiving." How does this verse instruct you to pray? How can this encourage you to pray at times that you may not feel like praying?

8. Read James 5:16b. What does James mean by a righteous man? Why is his prayer powerful and effective?

9. Reflect on the words of William Walford:
>   "Sweet hour of prayer, sweet hour of prayer,
>   Thy wings shall my petition bear

To Him whose truth and faithfulness
Engage the waiting soul to bless:
And since He bids me seek His face,
Believe His Word and trust His grace,
I'll cast on Him my every care,
And wait for thee, sweet hour of prayer."

10. Pray!

Chapter 6 – Learning to Trust

1. Read Hebrews 13:6. In what ways have you been confident in yourself alone, not trusting in God? How does this chapter lead you to change that? What are some specific things that you want to do differently? How can these changes affect your marriage?

2. Ephesians 1:18-19a says, "I pray also that the eyes of your heart might be enlightened in order that you may know the hope to which he has called you, the riches of his glorious inheritance in the saints, and his incomparably great power for us who believe." List five ways that you have seen God's hope and His riches and the work of His power evidenced in your past.

     1.
     2.
     3.
     4.
     5.

How do these verses and your list encourage you as you look at the present and to the future?

3. Read Psalm 112:7-8. What bad news do you fear? How does trusting God affect that fear? When has your heart been the most secure? Why? Over what enemy do you desire to triumph as you trust God?

4. The Psalms are filled with references to trust. Choose one of the following psalms (22, 37, 40, 56, 78, or 115) and list how the psalmist was demonstrating trust. Discuss how it correlates to your life now.

5. Hebrews 11:1 says that "faith is being sure of what we hope for and certain of what we do not see." Explain the difference between biblical hope and our "wishful thinking" hope.

6. Read Romans 15:4. What does it mean to wait patiently—knowing that God fulfills His promises?

7. Read Hebrews 11:1. What are you hoping for? Is your hope based on what God has said or is it based on what you can see?

8. "Praise be to the God and Father of our Lord Jesus Christ! In his great mercy he has given us new birth into a living hope through the resurrection of Jesus Christ from the dead, and into an inheritance that can never perish, spoil or fade—kept in heaven for you, who through faith are shielded by God's power until the coming of the salvation that is ready to be revealed in the last time. In this you greatly rejoice, though now for a little while you may have had to suffer grief in all kinds of trials" (1 Peter 1:3-6). How do these verses help you to have hope in a trial you are currently facing?

9. Share something in your life that you want to trust God for as you place your hope in Him who is faithful.

Chapter 7 – The Path of Righteousness

1. What do Galatians 3:28 and 1 Peter 3:7 tell us about eternal life? Is there a difference for men and women?

2. Wives have the awesome privilege of being Christ-like in their marriage. How can we choose to voluntarily submit as Jesus models for us in Philippians 2:4-8?

3. When is it difficult for you to submit? How can you allow God to help you overcome this difficulty?

4. The disciples had been arguing on the road to Capernaum about which one of them was first or greatest. Jesus sat the twelve men down, and said, "If anyone wants to be first, he must be the very last and be the servant of all" (Mark 9:35). What is Jesus teaching them—and us—about the contrast between earthly and eternal focus?

5. Micah 6:8 says, "He has showed you, O man, what is good. And what does the Lord require of you? To act justly, and to love mercy and to walk humbly with your God." Explain these character qualities God requires us to have in our lives. What are ways you can better exemplify these traits in your life?

6. Read Psalm 131. What "rest" do you hear in this Psalm? How does not being proud lead to trust and contentment?

7. What helps you to be independent in decision-making when your husband is away and then transition to allow him the role of head of the home when he is home? How can we encourage him in this headship role even when he is often away?

8. Read Ephesians 2:4-9. What did God do for us because of His great love for us? Explain "God raised us up with Christ and seated us with him in the heavenly realms." How does this benefit us now and for eternity?

9. What verse from this chapter did you find most meaningful? Why? Is there a change you feel God wants you to make in your life because of the truth of this verse?

Chapter 8 – True Friends and Lovers

1. How are things going in building a "best friend" relationship with your husband? Discuss ways you can be a better friend to him.

2. Read 1 Corinthians chapter 13. What do these verses say about the importance of love (especially verse 13)?

3. Reread 1 Corinthians 13 verses 4 to 8a. Which of the definitions of love are you demonstrating well in your marriage? Choose one aspect of love that you believe God wants you to improve on to deepen your relationship with your husband. How can you practically apply this to your relationship?

4. How would you suggest one could get the best advice about sexual intimacy? What are the biggest deceptions from our current culture concerning this topic? What Scriptures do you know that refute these lies?

5. Read Genesis 2:23 and 25, and 3:7. Why do you think Adam and Eve felt no shame initially? Why is there a difference in 3:7? What do you think these verses have to say about some challenges that arise in intimacy? How can "coming together" help in overcoming this secrecy and separateness?

6. Explain the principles found in 1 Corinthians 7:3-5. The normal God-given sexual drive is strong. According to verse 5, how might we be tempted if we deprive one another?

7. How do these verses confirm what author Don Meredith says in *Becoming One: Planning a Lasting, Joyful Marriage*, "God makes sex a sacrificial act that is redemptive, in that it gets my eyes off my needs and onto the needs of my mate?"

8. Read Hebrews 13:4. What is God asking you to do to honor marriage and your intimate relationship with your spouse?

9. What attitude or behaviors of yours could be hindering the enjoyment God intends for you in sexual intimacy? What attitudes or behaviors will enhance your physical relationship with your husband?

10. Plan a time to read the Song of Songs, preferably with your husband. Note what you learn from the expressions of love and intimacy in the ways the husband and wife relate to one another in their physical relationship.

Chapter 9 – Strength for the Storm

1. What are you struggling with or suffering with today?

2. What does Matthew 11:28-30 teach us to do with our burdens? How can you "rest" in Jesus despite hardships?

3. Read Matthew 14:22-31. Peter shows us how to weather the storm by keeping our focus on Jesus. He also shows us how to sink. What happens when we take our eyes off of Jesus and focus on the "storm" around us?

4. Share one thing that you have learned from this chapter about keeping your focus on God in the painful experiences of life.

5. Galatians 6:2 tells us to "carry each other's burdens, and in this way you will fulfill the law of Christ." How can you show Jesus' compassion to those who are hurting around you? How can your sufferings better prepare you to help others when they struggle?

6. The book of Job ends with Job "seeing" God through eyes of faith. He no longer just hears about God, but now he knows Him personally. This spiritual understanding allows Job to accept God's plan for his life—including suffering. How personally do you know God? What steps can you take to grow in your love and knowledge of God?

7. Read 2 Corinthians 12:7-10. Explain what Paul means when he states that he "delights in weaknesses, in hardships, in persecutions, in difficulties. For when I am weak, I am strong." How can we be strong even in adversity?

8. What can you do to build your relationship with your husband so that you are prepared to "lean on each other" in troubled times?

9. Thank God for His mercy and compassion as He is carrying you through hard times—using them for your good and His glory.

Chapter 10 – Healing for the Heart

1. What section of this chapter spoke the most to your heart and why?

2. Walter Wangerin Jr. said, "Forgiveness is a willing relinquishment of certain rights. The one sinned against chooses not to demand her rights of redress (rectify) for the hurt she has suffered." What do these words mean to you? Do you agree or disagree? Why?

3. Read Psalm 51:1-17. David wrote this psalm after the prophet Nathan came to him to confront David with his sins of adultery and murder. In what ways were David's sins harming him? How did he seek God for forgiveness?

4. In verse 51:4, David says he has sinned against God only. How does this verse remind us that when we hurt others it ultimately hurts God? When you ask others to forgive you should you also ask God to forgive your rebellion against His ordinances given to us to live by?

5. How do Joseph's words and actions in Genesis 50:15-21 show that he has forgiven his brothers for their sins—including selling him into slavery? What do you think allowed him to forgive and not seek revenge when he had the power to?

6. Ephesians 6:10-18 reminds us of who our true enemy is and how to do battle with him. What are the pieces of our "armor" and why is it crucial to have them on at all times?

7. Read Ephesians 4:31-32. Are your attitudes, your words, and your actions pleasing God and building relationships? Is there anything you need to "get rid of" or do to be kind, compassionate, and forgiving?

8. Read Psalm 103:1-3, 8. How does focusing on God's great love for us—including forgiving our sins—change us when we see our many undeserved blessings?

9. Allow God to examine your heart to show you if there is someone you have offended that you need to ask forgiveness of, or if there is someone who has offended you that you need to forgive. Without naming the person(s), ask others to pray for you to take the steps necessary to reconcile these relationships.

Chapter 11 – Grace and Gratitude

1. Read Romans 2:5-10. God will righteously judge each person according to what criteria? What will be the reward for of those who "persist in doing good"? What will be the fate of those who are "self-seeking and who reject the truth and follow evil"?

2. How does the certainty of your own judgment, one day, affect your desire to not let "willful sins rule" over you?

3. Acts 3:19 urges us, "Repent, then, and turn to God, so that your sins may be wiped out, that times of refreshing may come from the Lord." We are called to repentance—acknowledging our own sin and turning away from it. God graciously forgives and gives us refreshment. Ask God to reveal your areas of sin to you. Then repent and be refreshed!

4. Read Romans 3:23-24. Explain what "we are justified freely by His grace . . ." means in the context of this verse. How do these verses apply to you personally?

5. What do we learn from Mary about being a servant of the Lord in Luke 1:35? What was her response despite the personal cost? How willingly do you obey when God asks you to serve Him (or serve others in His name)?

6. In Mark 6:30-31 we find the disciples gathered around Jesus telling Him of "all that they had done and taught." They had been so busy that they hadn't even had time to eat! What was Jesus' invitation to them? What does this advice tell us that we need to do to take care of ourselves in order to be more effective in ministering to others?

7. Colossians 2:6-7 states, "So then, just as you received Christ Jesus as Lord, continue to live your lives in him, rooted and built up in him, strengthened in the faith as you were taught, and overflowing with thankfulness." Is thankfulness easy for you? When? When is it not? What practical steps does this verse suggest to move toward constant thankfulness?

8. Henri Nouwen stated, "Gratitude . . . goes beyond the 'mine' and 'thine' and claims the truth that all of life is a pure gift. In the past I always thought

of gratitude as a spontaneous response to the awareness of gifts received, but now I realize that gratitude can also be lived as a discipline. The discipline of gratitude is the explicit effort to acknowledge that all I am and have is given to me as a gift of love, a gift to be celebrated with joy." How can seeing that all you have in life is a gift from our lavish Lord help you to seek to develop a habit of an "attitude of gratitude"?

9. Ephesians 5:20 tells us, "Always give thanks to God the Father for everything, in the name of our Lord Jesus Christ." What is going well in your life now that you can thank God for? What problem are you having that you can thank Him for, knowing he is strengthening you through the difficulties?

10. What lessons from the tandem bike analogy help you adjust practically to your relationship with your husband in the sense of being a team?

Chapter 12 – Walking with God

1. Read Ephesians 2:8. What grace has God freely extended to you? How does fully understanding this motivate you to extend grace to others with your words and by your actions?

2. Share practical tips with one another such as cleaning tips and favorite "quick to prepare" healthy recipes.

3. Read Romans 8:28-29. Explain what it means to you to "know that in all things God works for the good of those who love him." What does it mean for you to be conformed to the likeness of His Son? How is that process going in your life?

4. Is there an area of your life that you desire to stop struggling with God over, instead telling Him "I'm yours" and submitting to Him? If so, spend time with God in giving this battle to Him. Ask others to pray for you to remain steadfast in being His.

5. Isaiah 45:9 (NLT) says: "What sorrow awaits those who argue with their Creator. Does a clay pot argue with its maker? Does the clay dispute with the one who shapes it, saying, 'Stop, you're doing it wrong!' Does the pot exclaim, 'How clumsy can you be?'" Discuss how it is sinful for us to think we know better than our heavenly Father, who is the Potter. (Isaiah 64:8: "We are the clay, you are the potter; we are all the work of your hand.")

6. Isaiah 7:9b cautions, "If you do not stand firm in your faith, you will not stand at all." How does this warning apply to us today?

7. Read 1 Timothy 6:6. What does this verse tell us about honoring God and focusing our desires on Him? (Read Philippians 4:11-12 if you wish to study another example of being content.)

8. What assurance do we find for strength on this path of life in Philippians 4:13?

9. What steps can you take, based on this chapter, to have the joy of a deep, vibrant, and consistent walk with your Lord? Pray and begin today to implement one step God has revealed to you.

Side by Side

Side by Side is a ministry to women who are married to medical and dental students, residents, or fellows, as well as wives of physicians and dentists. Affiliated with the Christian Medical & Dental Associations, Side by Side is a nondenominational, Bible-based ministry that is evangelical in nature. We seek to encourage, support, and minister to women in medical marriages through fellowship, Bible study, and prayer.

The purpose is based on "standing firm in one spirit, striving side by side" (see Philippians 1:27). We encourage standing by our husbands, striving with our sisters, and walking with our Lord.

Side by Side began in 1988 in Rochester, Minnesota, with six women meeting around a kitchen table. Today, there are chapters in twenty-five cities around the country. The women of Side by Side are from all over the world. They come from different backgrounds and different denominations, and they are in different stages of their husband's medical training. Some are physicians or dentists themselves.

Many women who come to Side by Side have never attended a Bible study before, while others may have been in Bible studies all their lives. The great thing is, that just doesn't matter! We have found a common bond in the fact that we are all in a medical marriage and the journey that is this medical life is much more fun when you have a companion.

For more information about Side by Side or to find out if there is a chapter near you, visit our website at www.cmda.org/sidebyside. You can also look us up on Facebook.

About the Author

Debby Read was born in the Midwest, then moved to Delaware at the age of five, where she was raised. There she met and later married Ed, her high-school sweetheart. The many good and also difficult experiences of her childhood gave Debby a desire to serve families by becoming a pediatric nurse. She attended the University of Delaware and received a bachelor of science degree in nursing. After her sophomore year, she married Ed, three days before he began medical school. After more than thirty-seven years of marriage, Debby is well acquainted with the life of a doctor's wife.

After graduation, she practiced nursing on a pediatric unit in Wilmington, Delaware, until Ed graduated from medical school. Debby and Ed moved to Jacksonville, Florida, for his internship and residency in the U.S. Navy. While living in Florida, they welcomed their first two children, Kristi and Kim. The Reads then spent two years on the island of Guam where their third child, Jon, was born. They returned to the U.S. and lived in Newport, Rhode Island, for Ed's last three years in the Navy. In 1985, they settled in State College, Pennsylvania, where Ed practiced full-time emergency medicine. There they enlarged their family in 1991 by adopting Jacob and David.

Together they learned a lot about teamwork in parenting and in encouraging one another in their church and community involvement. Debby kept her hand in nursing during these years teaching childbirth education classes and volunteering at the Pregnancy Resource Center. However, her favorite job was nurturing their five wonderful children.

In 2003, after sensing a strong call from God, Debby and Ed moved to Richmond, Virginia, to become area co-directors for the Christian Medical and Dental Associations' Campus and Community Ministries on the Medical College of Virginia campus of Virginia Commonwealth University. This has been a fulfilling and rewarding co-labor for them as a couple.

Debby's love of teaching is evident as she interacts with students at VCU, leads two women's Bible studies, and teaches children at her church. She especially enjoys mentoring women and the blessing of building relationships with them and the Lord. Together she and Ed strengthen their own marriage as they frequently do pre-marital and marital counseling. She loves spending time in the Word and growing in her love and knowledge of God.

Debby enjoys cooking and is often preparing food for students and for her family. She also enjoys visiting with friends, sewing, gardening, hiking, and reading. Kayaking on Lake Anna, where the Reads live, is a favorite shared pastime for Debby and Ed. They both love spending time with their children and their three precious grandchildren, Megan, Lauren, and Aiden.

Debby Read
305 Edgewood Drive,
Mineral, VA 23117
www.prescriptionforthedoctorswife.com

THE **BRIDGE** TO LIFE

You may have a lot of questions about trusting Christ as your Savior. Hopefully, the Steps listed below will help you to understand more clearly.

Step 1: God's Love and His Plan

Jesus said, "I have come that they may have life, and have it to the full"
(John 10:10)

God created us in His own image to be His friend, to experience a full life assured of His love, and to bring Him glory. But He didn't make us robots—He gave us freedom to choose to follow Him.

Step 2: Our Problem: Separation from God

The Bible teaches that God loves all men and wants them to know Him.

But man is separated from God and His love.

"God is on one side and all the people on the other side"
(1 Timothy 2:5)

Why is man separated from God and His love?

Because he has sinned against God.

"Your sins have cut you off from God"
(Isaiah 59:2)

"For all have sinned and fall short of the glory of God"
(Romans 3:23)

Where does this separation lead?

This separation leads only to death and certain judgment.

"Man is destined to die once, and after that to face judgment"

(Hebrews 9:27)

"Those who do not know God . . . will be punished with everlasting destruction and shut out from the presence of the Lord"

(2 Thessalonians 1:8-9)

But, there is a solution.

Step 3: God's Remedy: The Cross

Jesus Christ, who died on the cross for our sins, is the way to God.

"God is on one side and all the people on the other side, and Christ Jesus, Himself man, is beween them to bring them together, by giving His life for all mankind"

(1 Timothy 2:5-6)

"For Christ died for sins once for all, the righteous for the unrighteous, to bring you to God. He was put to death in the body but made alive by the Spirit"

(1 Peter 3:18)

Does this include everyone?

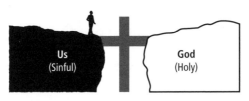

Step 4: Humanity's Response

Yes. But only those who personally receive Jesus Christ into their lives, trusting Him to forgive their sins, can cross this bridge.

"To all who received Him to those who believed in His name, He gave the right to become children of God"

(John 1:12)

"I tell you the truth, whoever hears my words and believes him who sent me has eternal life and will not be condemned; he has crossed over from death to life"

(John 5:24)

Jesus says, "Here I am! I stand at the door and knock. If anyone hears My voice and opens the door, I will go in and eat with him, and he with Me."

(Revelation 3:20)

How does a person receive Jesus Christ? Everyone must decide individually whether or not to receive Christ.

Believing means trust and commitment—acknowledging our sinfulness, trusting Christ's forgiveness, and letting Him control our lives. Eternal life is a gift we each must receive.

Jesus said, "You may ask Me for anything in my name, and I will do it"

(John 14:14)

Therefore, if you pray sincerely, asking Him this:

> Lord Jesus, please come into my life and be my Savior and Lord.
> Please forgive my sins, and give me the gift of eternal life.

—He will do it now.

Step 5: Assurance of Salvation

If you have invited Jesus Christ into your life, the Bible says you now have eternal life.

"He who has the Son has life; he who does not have the Son of God does not have life. I write these things to you who believe in the name of the Son of God so that you may know that you have eternal life"

(1 John 5:12-13).